My Life as an Army Wife

My Life as an Army Wife

☙

1954-1972

Edythe Price Gorman

ISBN-13: 9781534919419
ISBN-10: 1534919414
Library of Congress Control Number: 2016911074
CreateSpace Independent Publishing Platform
North Charleston, South Carolina

Dedicated to the love of my life

2nd Lt. William J. Gorman – 1953 Ft. Benning, Ga.

Originally, this book was just intended for my children, to give them some indication as to where they lived and attended school as "army brats," an affectionate term for army children. Then it occurred to me that other people may care to read about "my life as an army wife," so here it is!

Contents

CHAPTER 1

---·¢·---

Before Marriage

1945. WORLD WAR II was over!

This terrible scourge the world had experienced was finally finished, and there was a chance for life to return to normal. The troops were coming home; there were no more food stamps or gasoline rationing. The best part was my brothers-in-law were returning home. My oldest sister Felice's husband, Vince Tighe, came back from Germany, while Billy Monahan, my older sister Marie's husband, returned from Italy. Throughout the war, no one ever knew what might happen to the soldiers who were fighting. This fear hung over everyone's heads.

But now happy days were back. The family was together again in our hometown of Millburn, New Jersey. What a comforting feeling it was to have this normalcy again. I could breathe easier now that I knew these soldiers were home.

I was a sophomore in Millburn High and met a new student, Claire Sims. We became instant friends. Many days after school, we walked to Claire's home. Her mother, Mae Gorman Sims, was a sweet, happy, five-foot, plump Irish lady who always was singing old, mostly Irish tunes. We would drink sweet hot tea and eat sweet buns. We nicknamed each other "Bun" and still do use that name some sixty-five years later. When we finished our tea (we didn't use tea bags then—only loose-leaf tea), Mae would read our very convincing tealeaves from the bottom of the teacup. My romantic fortune usually went like this: I would meet a tall, handsome young man, attend a spectacular prom, and wear a ravishing dress. She would predict that I would fall in love with this young man and him with me and that we would have a wonderful life together. Sometimes, her fortunes included elaborate journeys and adventures. Mae had a fantastic imagination; we loved all her stories, both true ones and fiction. It always made me very happy to hear her stories.

Since Claire was an only child, I was always asked to join them so she had company. That was fine with me because I was like an only child—my sisters were eight and ten years older than I was. Occasionally, we would visit Gramma Gorman (Mae's mother) in Wharton, New Jersey. Claire and I stayed for a while then walked down to watch Wharton play baseball. It happened that Claire's first cousin was the short stop, Bill Gorman. Though not the grand event filled with ballrooms, tuxedos, and gowns that Mae often produced in her fortune telling, it was as significant an event in my life as anything she could have predicted.

Watching the baseball game was fun, and after the contest, we crossed the street to Claire's Uncle Henry's (Bill's father, whom we called Hen) confectionery store, where Claire introduced me to Bill. I thought, "What a cute guy!" He was five-feet-ten-inches tall with sandy, wavy hair—and most of all, those big, dreamy, blue eyes! I was instantly in love with him, but I knew I didn't have a chance with him since he had a steady girlfriend. We also lived too far apart. Ironically, Bill felt the same way toward me, but at that point, I had no idea about his feelings. So I didn't get my hopes up, but Claire and I were in the store numerous times. Somehow, we always seemed to end up in the store when Bill was there. We would talk, and I realized Bill had a great personality.

On August 22, 1948, Claire and I sat ready to watch another Wharton ball game when Bill walked across the ball field and said to me, "Hi, would you like to go into New York tomorrow night to see a Broadway show since my steady girlfriend has to work?" I was overwhelmed! I know I stared at him in disbelief.

I replied, "I have to ask my mother."

He immediately answered, "I already did, and she said 'yes.'" (He didn't even know my mother!) But Mae and Mom were friends, and she knew Mae's maiden name was Gorman. Also, I had already met the entire clan except Bill.

"Yes," I said happily. I could hardly contain myself. I was excited, nervous, and overwhelmed with happiness. I couldn't believe this was happening. It was as if this was a story out of one of Mae's tealeaf fortunes!

Bill's friend did the driving into New York along with his date. I knew both of them, so it relaxed me. We were all making small talk and laughing. *The Fourposter* was the name of the show, starring Betty Field and Burgess Meredith at the Ethel Barrymore Theatre. The show was excellent, and we had a great time on this double date.

On the way home, it was rather quiet. We had a little conversation, and with that, Bill put his arm around me. I snuggled right in, exactly where I belonged. Upon arriving home, I was about to reach for my front door when Bill put his arms around me, kissed me several times, and said, "I'll call you tomorrow night." I felt as if I was floating on air!

And he did, every night, sometimes twice from then on unless he was at my house. I'm sure at this point, we knew we were in *love*! What an overwhelming power! It's wonderful! It was love at first sight, something that is no longer believed in, but I know it is real because the course of our lives together was formed from that first meeting and then the date. It may be old fashioned, but that is perfectly OK with me because I am old fashioned. Now, I am not saying it must be love at first sight for everyone, but I know it worked for us.

Bill's friendship with his girlfriend came to a screeching halt. I truly felt sorry for her. This was the only unfortunate part of our relationship.

Bill and I saw each other as much as possible until he left for Mount Saint Mary's College in Emmitsburg, Maryland, in September. We wrote every day, never missed; plus, we made as many phone calls as we could. We were in as close to constant contact as was possible in those days.

Christmas 1948 came around, and it was time for me to meet Bill's mother, Ella, and Bill's sister, Peggy. I knew his father, Henry, from the store. Claire had warned me about Ella being strong willed and opinionated and having a bit of a temper! Was I nervous? You bet I was! I have been a bit of a nervous person my entire life. I have always dreaded certain situations, but I also never let that fear keep me from doing anything. A person has to face his or her fears, and I tried to face mine.

Ella was a robust woman with a five-foot-six, full-bodied figure, a round, full face, and a truly inviting smile. She gave me a wholehearted welcome, and I relaxed in her warm presence. Peggy, a teenager, was right behind her, sporting a wide smile. She was a true Irish beauty with curly red hair, peaches-and-cream complexion, and a loving personality to match. Peggy put me at ease immediately. All went well—I had now met his complete family, and they had all accepted me. I felt so much at ease and so happy.

This was an incredibly eventful time!

Not only was August 23, 1948, my first date with Bill, but also it was my first day of employment at Martindale-Hubble Law Digest as a clerk. I didn't stay there long, but I did meet Adele (Cookie) Corcoran, and we have been fast friends ever since.

While Bill was in college, I changed my employer to Ciba Pharmaceutical Company. My new job was in the order department. Then later, I had the opportunity to learn to be a telephone-switchboard operator. I enjoyed both positions, and one day I was asked to work in the New York office for the president of Ciba as a receptionist and switchboard operator in the Empire State Building! This meant I had to travel by train from Millburn, New Jersey, to Hoboken, New Jersey, and then continue by subway into New York City. This commute was not a problem because I knew my way around the city since my mother and I shopped in New York, enjoyed the Broadway shows, and naturally, the Radio City Music Hall.

The president's office was approximately on the seventy-ninth floor of the Empire State Building. I don't remember the exact number, but the staff showed me where the B-25 bomber accidentally hit the building in 1945. Many files were burned or destroyed. What a terrible time that must have been. (I can only think of how horrible it must have been for those poor people in the Twin Towers.) The story made me nervous, but I tried to ignore it.

Remarkably, I loved traveling in the elevators. While many people are afraid of them, I enjoyed the feeling.

The front office where I sat and the lounge had walls covered with exquisite light-blue silk with a little silver shimmer and birds in flight. What a beautiful sight! It was the kind of experience that I would read about in a book—the feeling of the sublime. I felt in awe of this magnificent environment.

While some days, the sky was clear, and I could see for a distance, most of the time I could not see Fifth Avenue because of the fog or clouds. I felt as if I was in a plane since the building would sway a little. That was a truly strange feeling.

This position was temporary because a full-time employee was needed. After the company conducted many interviews, none of the applicants was hired. As a result, I was invited to stay on permanently with a raise. Their offer was enticing and presented me with a serious dilemma. I had a plush job, the kind that many people wanted. It was something I enjoyed and could certainly have done well with it, but traveling in and out of the city in winter weather did not appeal to me. The long commute in good weather was one thing. But when I thought about how difficult it might be in a bad winter, I made my decision. I declined the position, but I thanked them for the opportunity.

I returned to my old job.

Christmas vacation was over, and Bill returned to the Mount. Time went slowly while he was away, but June 1952 finally came around, and Bill graduated from Mount Saint Mary's. He went directly to work at Picatinny Arsenal, a government installation, where he was employed during the summer months while in college. Things were really looking up but not for long!

✢

CHAPTER 2

We Are Married

WHAT A SHOCK! Bill was drafted into the military on August 22, 1952. Two months after graduation from college, PFC William J. Gorman started training at Camp Kilmer, New Jersey. After basic training, he was chosen for leadership school at Indian Town Gap, Pennsylvania. From there he went to Fort Benning, Georgia, for six months to attend Officers Candidate School (OCS). Bill graduated as a second lieutenant, infantry officer, US Army. This was outstanding! He was already an officer, and I was so proud of him. Bill had a thirty-day furlough, and he received orders for Camp Polk, Louisiana. We were so disappointed; we had hoped for the East Coast. It was one of the first lessons that I learned about life as a military spouse—you could be uprooted and moved around at any time. We were committed to that life.

Meanwhile, Bill and I talked about setting our wedding date, but we were sure all hell would break out from Ella, and then it did, big time. Ella did not want Bill and me to get married at that point, and she let it be known. I think she saw me as taking her son away, especially from the plans they had set for him.

I remember her saying to us at one point about being married, "Well, if you have to…" I was shocked at the insinuation, but Bill and I stayed above the nastiness as much as we could. We didn't have to get married; we wanted to be married. They wanted Bill to get out of the army when his obligation was fulfilled, work at Picatinny, build a house next to them, and get married, and everything would be wonderful. His family seemed to have his whole future planned out for him, almost as if he were still a little boy. But they were wrong! Bill informed them of our plans to stay in the army and then figure out our future; but we were sure living next door to Ella was not in our plans. They were outraged!

I couldn't believe how nasty the whole thing became. They just would not leave us alone. I was afraid that it might affect our coming marriage. After many phone calls and unpleasant letters, Bill had enough and laid the law down. He showed me how much he loved me by sticking up for us against his family. He confronted them and told them that we were getting married! He showed me that he was much more than a young man, that he had become an adult, and that we were both ready to commit to a lifetime together no matter what circumstances we would have to deal with or what the opposition to our being together might be.

But not everyone was against our getting married. My parents were thrilled and loved Bill; in their view, he could do no wrong. I knew this was a wonderful situation because so many parents of girls who were engaged did not approve of the husband-to-be, especially the girls' fathers. My parents saw him as responsible and wonderful. I was so happy about that.

We were engaged February 14, 1953. Mae had a huge bridal shower for me. Ella was upset because I didn't come directly to her before I greeted any of the other guests. Oh well! She had to learn that she was no longer the center of attention in Bill's life.

Claire was married, living in Illinois, and expecting their first child in March, so she could not travel safely. This was unfortunate, but it was something that everyone understood. At Claire's wedding, I was maid of honor and Bill was an usher. Naturally,

I thought she would be here for us, and I missed her so very much.

My dear mother made my beautiful wedding dress as she did for my sisters. I chose my dress from a magazine. It was available in a New York store, so Mom went into the city and copied the dress. It turned out perfectly. Mom was a proficient seamstress and had sewn wardrobes for fashionable, wealthy ladies traveling on cruise ships.

Our wedding was held on January 23, 1954, at Saint Rose of Lima Church, Short Hills, New Jersey, with a Mass at 10:30 a.m. Peggy was my maid of honor. Adele Corcoran and my high-school friend Jean Ennis were bridesmaids. Bill's best man was Bert Fenwick. Groomsmen were Bob Gorman, Ed Griffin, and Joe Murray. They were called ushers back then.

It was a cold but sunny day after a large snowstorm the day before. Everything was perfect, and our reception was held in the Millburn Inn. We honeymooned in the Roosevelt Hotel, New York City, for three days. Guy Lombardo and his orchestra serenaded us each evening—a lifetime memory. Just for a laugh, our room rate was $37.31, tax included, for two nights.

One thing that is very important to remember is that once we were together, Bill and I were always hand in hand whenever possible. I have known many married couples who seemed to lose the love they had as they aged, but Bill and I stayed in love our entire lives.

Back to Wharton, we packed and left the next day from Newark, New Jersey, by train to New Orleans, Louisiana. Both families were in Newark to wish us luck. Felice even made little sandwiches plus cookies for our trip, a marvelous sendoff. Our stateroom far exceeded our expectations. It was so much bigger than what we thought we would have—there was a room with a sitting area where we sat together, held each other, and watched the beautiful countryside go by.

The Gorman Family

The Price Family

CHAPTER 3

Camp Polk, Louisiana

AFTER THREE DAYS, we arrived in New Orleans, Louisiana, and then went by bus to Camp Polk, Louisiana. Dave, Bill's friend from Officer Candidate School, met us along with his wife, Lois, and drove us to our first home, 505 Curtis Street, Leesville, Louisiana. A furnished duplex with one bedroom was perfect for us. Plus, Dave and Lois lived across the street. While we were unpacking, they came over. Lois asked me if I brought my "flat," meaning my iron. We had a good laugh over that. Lois was from the New England states. Bill reported to work the next day to find he was officer in charge of the motor pool; that is where military vehicles are stored, repaired, cleaned, and generally maintained. He was not very happy with the orders. He was expecting something with more importance and a chance to show his abilities, but that would come in time.

But settling in wasn't just for Bill to receive his orders and his duties. My first order of business was that I had to have an identification card made stating my name and Bill's name, rank, serial number, and any other pertinent information. An ID card was essential to entering the post, the privilege of shopping, enjoying base activities, entering the Officers' Club, and when necessary, seeing the doctor or dentist. The Officers' Club, referred to as the "O" Club," is for officers ranked from lieutenant to general as well as chief warrant officers one through four. The noncommissioned personnel have their club, serving personnel ranked from private to sergeant, referred to as the NCO Club.

As the old saying goes in the service, you always have to know your "name, rank, and serial number." I learned that while it was Bill who was in the military, as an officer's wife, I also had responsibilities and a duty to be a good wife to him. It may seem odd to younger people, but life was this way for military wives then.

Almost immediately after arriving, we purchased our brand-new 1954 Plymouth car. It was right off the showroom floor. It happened to be the only one in a very small county agency, and we were very excited about it. It seemed like such a luxury. It was a beautiful sedan with a brown-and-cream exterior with a cream interior. Compared to other cars of the time, it was not large; but next to the typical car of today, it was huge. It was spacious and very comfortable. We were thrilled and felt as if we were floating as we drove home, feeling as if we were the only ones on the road.

Not everything that I saw, though, was beautiful and wonderful. Certainly, where I grew up had some poverty, but I had never experienced anything like I would in the South.

One morning I was looking out the kitchen window and saw an old beat-up garbage truck slowly moving along as several small black children ran from one garbage can to another, rummaging through them, mainly looking for bread. My very thoughtful father-in-law sent a Valentine candy box to me from his store. It was a bright-red, satin-covered, heart-shaped box with a big, red bow on top. Bill and I ate all the candy, naturally, so I put the empty box on top of the garbage can. I watched a little black African-American girl, no more than five years old, who was bare foot in a ragged dress with her dark, braided hair covered with white lint. She grabbed the box, holding it ever so tightly, and then ran to the truck, handed it to the driver (maybe her father), ran back, and continued searching. The scene was priceless. My heart went out to that poor little girl. I still think of her whenever I throw a piece of bread away…

It made me look at the world in a way I never had before. I realized that with the little that we owned, we still were so much more fortunate than those poor people were. These children ran from garbage can to garbage can, sometimes to find food for themselves, as I was later told, or sometimes to find feed for their chickens. They were from farming families and had so little money to get by.

It was odd that food seemed to be the center of so many events at that time.

Bill was coming home from the field, so to surprise him, I made a chocolate cake with vanilla frosting. I was so proud of my delicious-looking masterpiece. I carefully covered it with wax paper and left it on the table. Later that evening, I went into the kitchen, switched on the light, and found cockroaches crawling from under the wax paper! This freaked me out! I threw the cake out! What a disappointment that was. I had worked so hard, and I had no idea at all about the presence of the cockroaches. I was so angry—they were disgusting, and they had spoiled my surprise for Bill. But I would get over it. And I did.

Meanwhile, Bill had the opportunity to attend Aerial Observer School for one month, right on post. Bill was an infantry officer, so he was required to walk through dangerous swamp water, watchful of poisonous snakes, insects, and other dangers. He disliked this exercise intensely and always hoped to find something else. So when the opportunity came along to change his duties and direction, he jumped on it and loved everything about being a pilot.

During the day when Bill was in training or on duty, I kept myself busy by writing thank-you notes for our wedding gifts. As the sun went down, I'd get the heebie-jeebies thinking about the creatures that came out at night. I didn't have to worry about only the cockroaches and other insects and creepy-crawlies. Most of the houses were set up on stilts; this made it possible for homeless dogs and maybe hogs to collect under them. Growling, fighting, and crying would keep me awake. It was very frightening! What was especially scary was that not just the occasional dog was around, but packs of wild dogs roamed around wherever they wanted to go. These were not wild animals that had a natural fear of human beings. They were dogs that people had released, and they had formed into packs. I always worried about them, but I never had any direct problems with them other than having to listen to them under the house. Because I was frequently alone in the house, it did make me nervous.

Bill was in the field most of the time and home on weekends. I kept busy with various tasks, often household chores. And these chores, which would be easy to do today, were often very difficult in those times. Sometimes during the day, I would wash and iron Bill's heavy, two-piece, cotton, denim-like material fatigues. It wasn't easy since I was five foot two and 105 pounds, and these uniform parts were very substantial. In a small kitchen sink, they would be submerged into soapy water, and then the process would start: squeeze, rub, squeeze then wring, and keep wringing. I repeated this operation with clear water repeatedly in order to soak them in thick starch. Then it was time to maneuver this heavy, dripping uniform into my arms, run down two steps outside, and throw it over a clothesline. Then I once again squeezed and wrung the excess starch out. I would be soaking wet plus exhausted only to repeat this operation for the other half. If they were not dry, this meant I'd drag the kitchen chairs over a heating element or somewhere where they would get dry. Ironing these uniforms was a challenge, most of all the coveralls. When ironed to my approval, stiff as cardboard, they would be stretched out on the couch. They looked kind of scary, like either a mysterious person lying there or a stranger from outer space.

One good thing was that a small laundry truck would drive up the street several times a week, honking the horn. I would tie up our clothes and linens in a sheet, and the driver took them and returned everything washed, dried, folded, and sparkling clean for fifty cents. I was so grateful for this service. It made my chores a little bit easier.

I also had to look around the town for various items that were necessary. For example, Bill needed basketball shoes in order to join his company team. I entered the small shoe store in town, and an elderly male clerk greeted me. I inquired if the store stocked men's sneakers.

He replied, "No, madam, but we do have soft-shoe bedroom slippers." I almost laughed in his face, but I didn't. I thanked him and made a fast exit, and all I heard was "Thank you, madam. You all come back now." I must say Southern people were so gracious. Maybe I should have asked for tennis shoes! Oh well, I'm from Jersey!

Not long after that, I was invited to my first officers' wives coffee at the Officers' Club. It was really a command, not an invitation. I missed the first coffee. The next morning, Bill was called into the commander's office, who wanted an explanation as to my absence. I had a bladder infection, so Bill got off the hook. All officers' wives were expected to attend every coffee, tea, luncheon, and evening affairs with no exceptions! Unless a woman was giving birth or dying, she was expected to attend. This was a lesson to me about the serious nature of the lives of the officers' wives. Again, this may seem very odd to contemporary women, but in those days, it was the reality of the situation. The military could not do anything to me directly if I missed these events, but it would have had a very strong and negative impact on Bill's career. I had chosen to be his wife and to support him in his career, so I had to do what was expected of me as an officer's wife. If I had not followed the plan, it could easily have affected Bill's reviews and possible promotions.

Luckily, all the wives were very friendly, and they made me feel comfortable and welcomed into what easily could have been a difficult situation. I was worried about what might happen, but they were courteous and welcoming. They were able to help me become acclimated to this life, and they aided me in learning the requirements for being an officer's wife. This is what I learned:

The responsibilities of an officer's wife in 1954

A) Do not wear shorts, halter-tops, or hair curlers in public.
B) Coffees: casual dress, no slacks
C) Teas: hats, dress, stockings, heels, and *white gloves*
D) Always have your identification card on your person.
E) Stop at the guardhouse when entering the post and wait for direction. He may ask for an ID card, etcetera.
F) It is not appropriate for an officer to push a baby carriage or pull a child's wagon.
G) Nothing will be discarded on post grounds, i.e. candy wrappers, cigarette butts, gum.
H) Do not cut through a military convoy.
I) Do not draw attention to yourself.
J) Calling cards are required when invited to a senior officer's quarters for a social event such as dinner. When entering the quarters, place your calling card in the designated tray, one card for each adult residing in those quarters. A thank-you note should be sent the next day.
K) When going through a receiving line, shake hands with your bare right hand while holding the right-hand glove in

the left hand by the fingers so you're showing the cuff of your white glove.

L) There is a very good reason for all these social events, and it works, in order for all of us to get acquainted. Many longtime friendships came from this system. The men accomplish all this at work, but the wives needed day-time events. Evening events were the time to meet the spouses. It all worked well.

M) Post housings are referred to as quarters.

N) Post Exchange (PX): a department store for clothing, jewelry, household items, etcetera. ID is required.

O) Commissary (grocery store): show your ID upon checking out, place all items with the prices facing up in full view in order for the cashier to read correctly. Place in food groups, i.e. canned goods, meats, vegetables, etcetera with cigarettes last.

P) When you're in a vehicle during early morning on post, you will hear the bugler playing "you got to get up," that's reveille, while our flag is raised. You and any other passengers must exit the car. Stand at the car you're your right hand over your heart until the bugler is finished. Repeat in the same manner at dusk while our flag is lowered and the bugler signals "retreat" at the end of the day.

A general invitation was issued to all the officers' wives to attend a tea at the Officers' Club. I had never been to a formal tea anytime in my life, so I had no idea whatsoever what to expect. I dressed nicely and hoped for the best.

When I entered the room, I saw a splendid and somewhat daunting sight of many ladies dressed in their best clothes, as if they were going to church, all with hats and traditional white gloves.

The room was elegant, like the ballroom of a fine hotel. A long table was centered in the middle of the room and covered in a sparkling-white lace tablecloth, all topped with an elaborate fresh-cut-flower arrangement. Since this was a high tea, a beautiful china teapot, a pitcher for cream, and a china sugar bowl were carefully placed on a large silver tray along with small pastries and finger food in the middle of the table. Tiny mints in a silver dish completed the array. What a dazzling sight it was. I realized that I had a great deal to learn as an officer's wife.

I was a bit nervous about the new situation, but the other wives were very gracious and welcoming. They included me in small talk and made me feel at home. We received a cup of tea from an officer's wife, who was assigned to that duty for the afternoon, and she added cream and sugar to our liking. I helped myself to several pastries and continued to chat with the ladies.

I was so impressed with the tea that I could not stop telling Bill about it. I know that a high tea is not "his cup of tea," but he was interested because he loved me. We always tried to be interested in what the other was doing.

We were only stationed at Camp Polk for a few months when the orders were published: Camp Polk closing. All troops will go on maneuvers in South Carolina, and all dependents will move to Fort Riley, Junction City, Kansas. It was another lesson for me about life in the military—we could go almost anywhere at almost any time. No home in a single place would be permanent. I had to learn to adapt to new places and look at these changes as new adventures.

It was fortunate that the housing department had gone ahead and located housing off post for us. That was a relief. When I first heard about the orders, I was worried about finding new housing, so this helped a great deal. It was tough for the families with kids and animals. So here we go—time for another adventure!

The designated day arrived! We put everything in the car that we owned, even my little houseplant, and drove out to camp, dropped Bill off, and said our good-byes. I drove out to Kansas, a two-day trip. The saying "camp follower" was appropriate for me right now.

Lois was driving her car ahead of me, so that worked well. We had cleaned out our refrigerators earlier, and at noon, we pulled over to the side of the country road and had our picnic with the cows looking over the fence at us intently, watching us eat our food as if we were aliens visiting their world. This was something very few people would do in today's world, but it was so much fun. I didn't have a car radio, but Lois did. When we'd stop, she'd inform me of the Sen. Bobby Kennedy/Jimmy Hoffa Teamster investigation. It seemed as if many important events were going on in the world.

Flight School – Camp Rucker, Al.

CHAPTER 4

---⋄---

Fort Riley, Kansas

THAT NIGHT WE stayed in a small motel. They were all small in 1954. Having never been in a motel without our spouses, we locked the one and only window, pushed the dresser against the door, put our wallets under the pillows, and attempted to sleep. We both tried to pretend that we were perfectly fine, but we were like two scared birds, acting as if we were comfortable and happy. Putting on a good face helped with the nervousness.

Arriving in Junction City, Kansas, we drove to my assigned apartment. It was a four-apartment row house. Our apartment was the second one in, next to the owner/manager Max Geis. I found the rooms very clean, with the kitchen, living room, dining room, and bedroom and bath upstairs. The first to greet me was Virginia Colborne, yelling, "My name is Virginia, but call me Virgin for short." She was a jolly person, always making me laugh, and she had a heart of gold. Virginia told me I was pregnant after I confided in her as to how nauseous I was every morning. I was so happy and so anxious to tell Bill.

Bill finally returned. As I waited, I saw him gingerly walking toward me with his pants legs rolled up to his knees, carrying his boots along with the rest of his gear. He had contracted poison ivy from soaking his feet in a river. I felt sorry for him, but I had to smile because he looked so funny! I had to tell him right away about how I was feeling and Virginia's opinion.

We had to wait a few days until Bill's feet had healed before we saw the doctor. He lived in a big, white southern home, and the dining room had been turned into the examination room. It was like something out of a movie. He was also gentle and very polite, like the image of a southern gentleman. After examining me, he did confirm I was "expecting." We were both thrilled!

Things seemed to be going along very well, with almost no incidents to speak of. Then, one very hot night in Junction City, Kansas, with seemingly not a breath of air, drama erupted. All the neighbors sat outside, eight of us plus kids, on lawn chairs. We were all talking, laughing, and having a great time. All of a sudden, Max, our landlord, came storming out of his apartment, waving his Bible. "You're all evicted."

We all looked at one another in disbelief! Dave and Lois were there also, and David shouted, "You cannot evict us; we don't even live here!" With that, Virginia stood up, pointing her finger right at Max and proceeding to rant and rave at him at the top of her lungs! Old Max quickly vanished. We never knew why this happened, maybe because we were in the Bible belt and we were Yankees. Maybe he simply didn't like a large group of people sitting outside and being happy. I really don't know.

This part of the United States is where the movie house will not open until the congregation comes out of church. Even though I came from a religious family and area, it was not as serious as it was there.

But we did not let this strange event bother us. We continued sitting there while Bill told jokes, his favorite pastime. Since he grew up in a candy store filled with all kinds of people, there was a new joke every day. Soon after Max left, Virginia and her husband insisted we move in with them. She didn't want us to pay any more rent to Max, and so we did. We looked for another apartment while we stayed with Virginia and Walter, plus their teenage daughter, "Little Virginia," and two toddlers, Cathy and Chrisy, for about two of the most comical weeks. We'll never forget sharing a very small apartment that comfortably fit two people, not seven squeezed in together.

Luckily, Bill received orders for flight school at Gary Air Force Base in San Marcos, Texas. Even though Bill was in the army, he went to an air force base. The doctor suggested I should fly home to New Jersey while Bill drove. We had a few weeks leave saved, so we drove to the airport. Never having been on a plane, I was terrified, but I didn't want Bill to know; he was concerned already since I was going alone. Flying would be one more fear I had to face—something it seems we all have to do in our lives. I was nervous; my hands were sweaty, and my heart was pounding. But I pulled up my courage and got onto the airplane. It was a small plane in comparison to planes today. I boarded the airplane, and Bill started for New Jersey.

The trip, however, did not go without a hitch. After a short time, the passengers were ordered off the plane while they made some sort of check on the plane. They never told us why. Then after about an hour, we boarded again. This time we actually took off. I had just started to get comfortable and had begun to release my tight grip on the seat when lightning started. And it was not just a few bolts of lightning and then over with. That would have been too easy. Instead, it became a severe storm. The plane was shaking, and there was incredible lightning and horrendous thunder. As the storm worsened, the plane unexpectedly dropped a couple of feet. Most of the passengers were vomiting all over. With that commotion, all of the luggage above us came tumbling down, hitting most of us on the head. What a mess! Some of the women were hysterical. I was so scared because I thought the plane would go down, and I had just become pregnant! The luggage kept sliding back and forth in the aisle until we finally landed at the Newark, New Jersey, airport. Both families were shocked when they saw me. Pale, weak, and shaking, plus I was exhausted! I am sure they also noticed the offensive odor coming from my clothes. When we arrived home, a hot bath was definitely needed. While falling into bed, I thanked the dear Lord for my safe arrival.

The next day Bill arrived in Wharton. Stopping once at a motel, he couldn't sleep, so he continued. Most of the time he drove with his handkerchief wrapped around the steering wheel. Since the car didn't have air conditioning, it must have been brutal. Our visit with the family was very pleasant, but now it was time to move on to Camp Rucker, Alabama, for flight school. Bill was so excited!

Meanwhile I miscarried. I did not experience any real pain physically, but of course, mentally this was a terrible thing. We were both very disappointed because we wanted children as soon as possible. Luckily, life was busy, so I did not have time to dwell on this misfortune. We had to move on with our lives, and we were both convinced more babies would come in the future, God willing.

CHAPTER 5

Gary Air Force Base, Texas

TRAVELING TO TEXAS was an adventure for us. While eating in a different restaurant every meal and trying to find a hotel wasn't easy, it was fun. I'm sure Bill got tired of me saying, "Honey, look at that," over and over again. I was like a little kid. I was so excited by every new sight that I couldn't contain myself.

The country was overwhelming as we drove through it, constantly changing. Sometimes there were flatlands, sometimes forests, sometimes cities, and sometimes mountains. We were approaching Chattanooga, Tennessee, and I suggested we should see Lookout Mountain, a panoramic view of seven states. It seemed like such an exciting thing to do. How often does a person have the chance to see a magnificent landscape from such a height? Bill was not too keen about this idea, but we went anyway. It felt as if we were taking off in a very slow airplane as the car kept climbing—straight up, up, up. At one point, I thought the car would tip over backward. I didn't mention that on my side of the car, a TV antenna was tied down; it went the full length of the car and was heavy, so it seemed as if it might make the car topple over. We were carrying it because my parents had given us a small TV set. This was a huge luxury—our own TV set and an antenna!

When we finally reached the top and checked the price to enter, we were shocked. We were, of course, as a young, newly married couple, watching our money. We both wanted to go in to the park, but after much consideration, we decided not to. And it didn't matter because we had a magnificent view right where we stood anyway! It was the most extraordinary view that I could have ever dreamed of seeing! The advertising was correct—we were able to see seven states. Normally, such a height might have made me nervous, but I was just taken in and overwhelmed by the sheer beauty of the view. I could see towns in the distance in valleys that looked so small that they seemed to be part of a model-railroad exhibit. I felt as if I was in the presence of God there. It was truly awe-inspiring. I think this is the feeling that the Romantic poets used to call the sublime—something that inspired true awe, and it did. I felt so small in the presence of such beauty but comfortable and happy there.

After a while though, it was necessary to leave and continue our journey. Now we faced the dreaded ordeal of driving down, down the hill!

We started creeping down the hill slowly because Bill was definitely concerned about the car holding up, especially the brakes. I was saying over and over, "Oh, my God."

Bill yelled over to me, "Pray the brakes hold!" I prayed as much as I could, and I tried to do something to help. So with the window down, I reached up and held onto the antenna, like that would help. I envisioned the antenna breaking free and sliding down the hill ahead of us! We were both shaking at the bottom of that horrendous undertaking. It felt as if it must have taken hours for us to get to the bottom of the hill, but I am sure it was only ten or fifteen minutes. Bill pulled over to relax and check the car. We both broke into laughter! Every time I told that story, Bill gave me that "look" with a grin.

Once we arrived in San Marcos, Texas, we stopped in to see Lois and Dave. He was in flight school also. They lived in a very small house and were not very happy with it. We started looking for housing, the first being a small, unpainted, wooden house with a dirt floor and outhouse! Bill and I rolled our eyes at each other. No thanks! It was a shack right out of the western movies. We did, however, did rent a tiny apartment that was adjacent to an old farmhouse in New Braunfels. It had a galley kitchen, sitting room, and inside plumbing but no shower, just a very old antique tub. It sounds quaint now, but it was far from ideal. Water bugs lived in the bathroom! They were two inches long, plus cockroaches (nocturnal also) made our acquaintance. As far as I was concerned, it wasn't very relaxing in there at night. Nighttime was definitely not the time to take a bath!

It was a strange environment and took me a while to get used to it. I was so lonely there that I could not wait for Bill to return about five o'clock. One day, the farmer's wife—that sounds funny—came over carrying a hot chicken dinner with dumplings. What a treat! It reminded me of an orphan child from a Charles Dickens novel. Thank God that housing arrangement didn't last too long.

Lois found a large rental house close to town, and the four of us moved in together. It worked out perfectly. It was a summerhouse with big rooms and a garden. As we were moving in, I noticed an ironing board built in the wall. I pulled it down, and out dropped cockroaches. Oh no! In the corner was a white cockroach; we figured it must be the queen. Dave killed it anyway!

We were not there very long when Dave didn't pass the check ride, a flight examination. Because he failed the test, he was given different orders; they left for another post. It was sad. Lois and I had been very good friends. I really missed her.

But because of the housework and the visits from other pilots and their wives, I did not have time to stay lonely for long. We had many good times since Bill's pilot friends came over to study. The wives came along to talk very quietly. It was Thanksgiving.

The girls had come over the day before, and we peeled, sliced, and diced all our favorite foods for our big meal. All I had to do the next morning was stuff the bird, and into the oven it went! The group arrived with more goodies—desserts, side dishes, everything we could have wanted for a wonderful holiday meal. We all had a great day, just like home. Several hours later, we all took a stroll to the park and river just a short way down the dirt road. Most of us sat at the river's edge with our feet dangling in the Guadalupe River, watching the fish and telling stories. Then back to the house to eat again. What a perfect day it had been. A good time was had by all.

Christmas was nearly here. That meant we would be headed for Camp Rucker, Alabama.

CHAPTER 6

Camp Rucker, Alabama (1954)

WE PULLED INTO Camp Rucker at dusk, and very few lights were on. There were no troops. It was eerie and felt like something out of an end-of-the-world movie. It was so strange that we returned the next day. During the day, we were able to see troops and find the housing building. We were assigned a house on stilts again, referred to as "splinter village," but this time there were rows of them, mostly for pilots. That was fun! We got to meet lots of fine people. I was pleased to find that there were many happy couples.

Well, we had a house, but we had absolutely no furniture. Such a dilemma! In town, we found a small furniture store, but we didn't want to buy any, so we convinced the owner it would be in his best interest to rent furniture. The bewildered man didn't have a chance with two fast-talking northerners. It worked out well, though, for everyone. We were able to rent the furniture we needed, and the owner of the business did very well after having us as customers. We let the other couples know about his store, and they gave him a great deal of business. Change can be a good thing for everyone if it is done with mutual benefit in mind.

We also had wonderful news, the best possible! We were going to have a baby. We were thrilled. The news was so wonderful, but the way we got it was less than joyous. Going to an army clinic to be tested was an experience. It was something I did not enjoy. There was a line to fill out all the paperwork, another line with about twenty ladies for blood pressure, and another line for weight, height, and finally my physical exam. After I was dressed, one of the doctors spoke on nourishment and weight gain. The army's policy on weight gain was there should be no more than twenty pounds. If the doctor decided I was gaining too much at any given time, into the hospital I would go! Many of the pregnant wives kept a toothbrush and toothpaste in their handbags. We never knew!

Bill was so excited to start flying at Rucker but also apprehensive. Classes started by having the men placed in groups, and each group had a different color hat—Bill's was green—like a baseball cap that they wore every day. On each hat was pinned a small, silly looking bird. As the men completed one phase, the pin was moved clockwise on the cap until it made a full circle. Of course, each phase was more of a challenge.

During this time, we met LaDonna and Chuck Rodgers. Immediately Bill nicknamed him "Buck" from Buck Rodgers, the old comic strip about a space adventurer. Bill was called "Stormy" since he flew in a sudden storm.

The four of us had a day's outing, driving to Panama City, Florida. It was a beautiful, sunny day and the gulf was a gorgeous color blue, nothing like we had ever seen before, with miles of sandy beaches. No hotels existed there at that time in 1954. We spread our blanket out and were ready to eat our picnic lunch, but suddenly, the wind blew sand all over us and unfortunately, our picnic lunch. Like a flash, we were out of there with our mouths full of sand! This evacuation was done with the speed and efficiency that the army would have been proud of!

LaDonna was also expecting her first baby, so we had a lot in common. It gave us much to talk about. We spent many hours planning for our babies: what we would do, how we would decorate, what kind of things we would need. This was truly comforting.

Life on the post was easier in many ways than I might have expected. In order to see a movie on post, all we needed was twenty-five cents each. Buck claimed that Bill only went in order to see the *Road Runner* cartoon. I agreed. When we were still at Camp Polk, by the end of the month, because payday was only on the last day of the month, we would search our pockets for twenty-five cents. We ate Spam the last couple of days. Now that Bill collected flight pay, life had improved, and we were able to make a few purchases to help our lives and circumstances. A sewing machine was one such item.

Most girls grow up with their mothers in the kitchen. Not me. I grew up around my mother at the sewing machine and loved it. I must note that my mother was also an excellent cook, but her love of sewing stuck with me the most. After checking out the ready-made made maternity clothes in town, it was time to purchase our first sewing machine. Bill and I enjoyed playing with the different gadgets and do-dads. In the South, fabric was inexpensive because of so many cotton mills. This abundance allowed me to sew a great deal of clothing. I loved doing it.

The weather in Alabama was beyond hot, plus the humidity was unbelievable. I thought I had learned about heat in Texas, but this was much worse. Being a Yankee and used to the weather in the northeast made me extremely uncomfortable in this tropical heat. It was so humid that it was always impossible to get dry. We only had one little fan, and that didn't help. In the middle of the night because the sheets would become saturated with sweat, we would get up, strip the bed, and make it again with dry sheets. We'd douse one another with baby powder. Then we would try to sleep again, but in minutes, we were dripping wet! It was so difficult to get a good night's sleep. The next day after showering and putting on his uniform, Bill would be soaking wet; it was awful.

I experienced something there that I never thought I would. In fact, I was shocked by it because it showed the poverty that existed there. Every morning an African-American girl (looking for work) would very softly knock on the door. She said that she would do anything: clean the house, iron, babysit, and even wash the car for fifty cents a day. Also, she would eat anything available with our consent, but we had to keep an eye on any liquor in the house, mainly gin. I could hardly understand anything she or any other poor African American said at first. Their dialect and accents were very thick. But I paid attention and realized that they were hard working and were simply trying to find what work they could. Eventually, I got the hang of understanding their speech.

Before graduation, the pilots were obligated to fly cross-country. They were only gone a short time when our neighbor Betty Westlake, whose husband Ed was also a pilot, went into labor. I felt so sorry for her because none of us girls could stay in the army hospital with her. I think it would have been better for Betty if we could have remained with her. It was the army's policy, and those were very different times from today. It all worked out though. She gave birth to a healthy little girl. Ed soon returned from the trip, but he missed all the excitement. That didn't make him any less a proud daddy though. He was beside himself with happiness and excitement.

On graduation day, all the pilots and their wives stayed in the army guesthouse. It sounds very grand and luxurious, but it was far from that! Rather than being some kind of a well-appointed facility, it was a long, bare building. Inside were rows of bedrooms on each side of the hall, with only two bathrooms. A very heavyset African-American woman, the guesthouse overseer, sat at a desk halfway down the hall. A radio on the desk was blaring with Rev. Billy Graham's voice as he preached. She sang while waving her arms in the air and yelling, "Hallelujah!" I had to smile as I admired her strong faith.

Betty, Ed, and baby Wendy Westlake stayed in the room next to us. The men were not there when Betty put the baby in the middle of their bed and tucked sheets all around her, completely safe. Betty knew the pilots' wives and I would hear Wendy if she made a peep!

Betty left the room, and when she returned a few minutes later, she found the bed stripped clean and *no baby!* She panicked! She ran down the hall, yelling and crying, "Where is my baby?"

Some of us were running behind her, also in a panic. But thankfully, it didn't last long. Just a few seconds later, little baby Wendy was found in the laundry cart, unhurt and surrounded with sheets. None of us could figure out how a maid could not notice the baby. Naturally, it took Betty a while to calm down. We all sat there and tried to console Betty and each other.

Soon after, a rumor was going around Bill's class that we were all going to Germany. We would be happy with those orders. It would have been exciting to go overseas and comforting to go to a place like Germany where we knew the country was modern. But when Bill received his orders, they were for helicopter school. So unfortunately, it was back to Gary Air Force Base in Texas.

Graduation on April 2, 1955, was a proud event for all of us as each pilot received his certificate from the commander that stated he was officially a pilot. At that time, ladies were called upon to pin the silver wings over the left breast pocket of the pilot's uniform. It was exciting, but that wasn't the end. The commander presented each lady with miniature wings. What a surprise, and this token was very much appreciated.

Bill was promoted to first lieutenant; he now wore silver bars on his shoulders, replacing the second lieutenant gold bars. Along with the promotion came a pay increase; that was always appreciated. There was a downside, however. Bill received orders for Korea in August. What a shame; we had hoped for Germany.

CHAPTER 7

──────── ✢ ────────

Gary Air Force Base, Texas

THERE WE WERE, back at Gary Air Force Base once again. It seemed as if we were living a life of human ping-pong, moving back and forth between bases! This time we lived in a small motel in San Marcus for six weeks. The living space was tight and cramped; but since we didn't know the specifics of our next living arrangements, it seemed best to be able to move whenever it was necessary.

Bill was concerned every day about passing the course since a helicopter was much more difficult to maneuver than an airplane. So he studied and readied himself with a fierce intensity and dedication.

Luckily, we knew a couple there. Wally and Aloma Blaisdell were in the next efficiency apartment with their two-year-old daughter, Karlin. We knew them from Camp Rucker. Wally and Aloma were both from Hawaii, so he used to demonstrate how fast he could climb a palm tree. It was very impressive! And the four of us spent a great deal of time together when we could.

Since we had the chance, on weekends, we would travel to some point of interest; the Alamo in San Antonio was the first. It was surprising though to actually see it. From the *Davy Crockett at the Alamo* movie with Fess Parker that had just come out earlier that year, I thought that the building was much bigger than it actually was. I guess that is a lesson about the power of imagination from movies and TV. I do remember that some of the time, I had the music from the "Ballad of Davy Crockett" going through my head as we walked around. Nevertheless, knowing all the killing that took place on the exact spot where we stood was a deeply moving experience. It is interesting that a small spot in the world can have such a large impact on national events. Who would have believed that a tiny church turned into a fort would become a rallying cry for American troops? Who would have believed that so many famous Americans of the day—Jim Bowie and Davy Crockett, among the most well-known—would die there? Even though it was a small space physically, it had enormous impact on us.

We also had the pleasure of visiting the Japanese Tea Garden. It was such a beautiful and lovely place. There were exquisite flowers and shrubberies, all very ornate. Not a blade of grass was out of place, and serene Japanese music played softly in the background. It was a reflection of the Japanese approach to nature; a human environment must be made to fit with the surroundings in a harmonious fashion. Our afternoon was educational and peaceful. This was a quiet and calming time, and I was grateful for it. It felt like a calm in the midst of a storm.

We were anxious to have our baby, but every day meant we were one day closer to Bill's departure for Korea. So much was going to happen almost at the same time, and these events would affect our family profoundly in both positive and negative ways. Bill and I were both aware that sad and happy times were coming.

It was time to leave Texas and return to splinter village at Camp Rucker for Bill's second phase of helicopter training and graduation. This time we drove the southern route by way of New Orleans, along with Aloma, Wally, and baby Karlin. Approaching the French Quarter, we saw an artist's delight as we looked up at the large, old, three-story hotels with the wrap-around balconies.

I could only imagine how all this would look at Mardi Gras with flirtatious ladies up on the balconies, throwing colorful necklaces down to the large, yelling crowds, plus all the bizarre costumes and very loud music. It would be such fun!

We had dinner in an old hotel, which was very charming. It was one of those grand buildings in the French Quarter, about three stories high and very beautiful. Ornate cast-iron railings (with a whirling floral pattern that seemed almost too delicate to be made from such tough material) lined the long porches of all three floors. The building was an old but very clean brick building, and floral arrangements hung every few feet on the cast-iron railings.

The inside of the hotel was also exquisite. The room was seemingly simple, but the tables were set with fine tablecloths and the best linen. The walls had what looked like old European paintings adorning them. It was such a lovely place.

Like the surroundings, the food was also excellent. I would have expected this kind of food in a five-star hotel in New York City. The men ordered steaks, and the ladies had seafood. Unfortunately, because of my pregnancy, I did not have any alcohol, but I did have a delicious southern sweet tea. Because we were traveling and had to be cautious about bathroom facilities, we decided not to try any Cajun food. We didn't need anyone on the trip having stomach issues from spicy meals.

Because this was New Orleans, we could never be sure about what might happen. When the waitress, a pretty girl, gave us the bill, her comment to Bill and Wally went something like this: "Get rid of the ladies, come back, and I will show you a good time." There I sat, eight months pregnant, and Aloma was holding Karlin! We all looked at each other in disbelief! Once outside we all had a good laugh, and then Aloma and I kept teasing the men.

The next morning we walked across the street where the starving artists had their artwork hanging on a fence. It was a large display of many kinds of paintings, ranging from oils to watercolors and landscapes to portraits to images of New Orleans. As much as it felt as if we were in a large, outside museum, we had to cut our art seeing short. Just as we began to be involved in looking at the paintings, a gigantic swarm of mosquitoes descended from out of nowhere! It was like an attack from a bad science-fiction movie. Perhaps it could have been called *The Giant Mosquitos Invade New Orleans*!

But we were saved. Several strangers walked over to Karlin and after asking permission, smeared their anti-mosquito cream on her legs and arms. Aloma was most thankful for these caring people. It showed the graciousness of so many of the southern people I met. It was almost like Blanche Dubois in Tennessee Williams's *A Streetcar Named Desire* when she says that she has "always depended on the kindness of strangers." Well, we did not always depend on it, but this time the strangers' help with the little girl was deeply appreciated.

CHAPTER 8

Camp Rucker, Alabama

Just as Bill predicted, flying a helicopter was much more difficult than flying a plane. This was a completely new experience for him, and he had a great deal of information to learn in a very short time. So he buckled down and applied himself. It was inspiring to see how hard Bill worked and studied. I was so proud of him.

The time went fast, and I managed to gain more weight; I waddled around. It started to feel as if I had a giant beach ball inside me. I was starting to really feel the pregnancy now.

Bill graduated from helicopter school on July 9, 1955. It was such a joy to see him relieved and happy—school was over. Then it was back on the road to Jersey.

Debra Ann Gorman

Bill in Korea - 1955

CHAPTER 9

New Jersey and Korea (1955)

BILL RECEIVED HIS orders to go to Korea as part of the 7th Aviation Company, Korea. He flew the H-13 helicopter for this deployment. When Bill got these orders, he could have requested a thirty-day extension. The more we discussed that possibility, the more it seemed best to decline. That way he would not miss the baby's second Christmas. Bill had two very special holidays that he cared about the most: Christmas and Saint Patrick's Day.

There we were at the Newark, New Jersey airport, August 20, on a Saturday night with both families, and I was nine months pregnant and as big as I could possibly stretch. Knowing he'd be away for fourteen months was heart wrenching. We all put on a grand act, smiling, kissing, and being silly while saying our goodbyes; but it was a very difficult challenge because I couldn't stop thinking about us being apart. My heart was hurting for him because he had to leave all alone while I had many supporters. I think he needed me as much as I needed him. After all the time we had spent together, I just couldn't believe that we would be separated for so long—and now of all times. At a time like this, couples should be together, but I knew I had signed up for this life as the wife of a US Army officer.

My labor pains started August 23, seven years after our first date. While the beginning of the labor seemed punctual, the actual process was long and exhausting. I was in labor for thirty-two hours in a room with no air conditioning. The heat and humidity alone would have made it difficult, but adding delivering a child to the mix made it almost unbearable. As I was going through the labor, my mother stood by my side and rubbed the cramps in my legs. She was so loving and persistent in her efforts to help me. I don't know how she did it for so many hours, but she proved to be a very strong woman and a wonderful mother. God bless her.

Finally, exhausted, soaked with sweat, and beyond feeling any more pain, I heard the most beautiful sound of my new baby crying—she was alive and well.

On August 24, 1955, Debra Anne Gorman arrived at Overlook Hospital, Summit, New Jersey: eight pounds, eleven ounces, with blond hair and blue eyes, and she was very healthy, thank God. Hen made numerous phone calls to army personnel to locate Bill and finally did when he was about to ship out. Hen proudly announced the birth of Debra to Bill; that removed his worries.

Soon after a very excited new father called me in the hospital. He was overjoyed to know we were both fine. This phone call was like none we had ever had before; we laughed, cried, and kept repeating how much we loved each other. It was the longest phone call we had ever made, and it seemed as if we were on the phone forever. When we hung up, I felt reinforced; I had really needed to talk with him. Even though we were far away from each other, it seemed as if Bill was in the room with me and that we would always be together.

While Bill was away, Debbie and I split our time between Wharton and Millburn since I did not have a home of my own. Debbie was the first grandchild for Ella and Henry, so they could not get enough of her. Ella and Peggy argued as to who would give her a bath or get her from her nap. I did some sewing for Peggy and helped with cleaning and other housework, but basically, I was bored. Ella wanted to care for Debbie so I could go to work. Oh no, I wasn't about to leave Debbie. Sometimes in the evening after Debbie was in bed, I'd help Henry at the store, cleaning the candy case, straightening greeting cards, and talking to Bill's friends. It was a very nice night out for me.

Then in Milburn, I had my parents plus my sisters and their families. They both had had babies in the last year. Felice had two older boys, Mick and Bruce, and then baby Suzanne. Marie had Tim and Kathleen and then baby Karen. There was always something going on that made the time move along. Adele was married in the spring; that was a joyful time and picked up my spirits.

Bill went on R&R (rest and relaxation) in Japan, and he had quite an amazing shopping spree. Debbie received a large, elegant Japanese doll dressed in fine silks. My gift was a magnificent K. Otsuki pearl necklace and earrings. Bill also gave me yards of silk material in three different colors with evening bags of the same material. My mother made evening dresses out of the material for me. Bill even sent a complete set for twelve settings of Noritake china. This was all a wonderful surprise!

Bill wrote from Korea that Rita Moreno, the movie star, arrived in Korea to entertain the troops. He had the pleasure of escorting her to the latrine (outhouse) and standing outside while she utilized the accommodations. I assume there wasn't any running water and no hand sanitizer (not on the market in 1956). What did she do? Maybe if she reads this book, she will let me know. Want to bet?

We didn't have computers or e-mail, but thank God, we wrote every day. Bill did get one call through from Japan. Bill said, "Hello, Doll, over."

I replied, "Hi, honey, over."

Originally, Bill called me Baby Doll, but he shortened it to Doll because of the brevity of these conversations. We were not allowed much time. And that's how the conversation continued. All the time my voice was on a loudspeaker! Needless to say, it was a difficult conversation but so marvelous to hear his voice. Simply the sound of his voice, after being apart, made me so happy.

It was finally the day—Bill was coming home in December 1956. We were so excited while Hen was driving us into New York LaGuardia Airport. I was trembling the entire time. My shaking only stopped when I saw him, and he wrapped me in his arms, both strong and loving. I was in paradise! Initially Debbie was not fond of this man with her mother, but that changed very quickly. She fussed at first, but then both Bill and Debbie fell in love with each other.

Bill had received orders for Yuma Test Station, Yuma, Arizona. We had hoped for his placement somewhere on the East Coast, but that didn't happen. Really, just being together was enough. We managed to visit every relative and friend before we left since they had not seen Bill for fourteen months. Also, we didn't know how long we'd be in Arizona.

We naturally made a trip to say good-bye to my favorite, most special Aunt Bea and her husband, Uncle Freddy. Debbie and I had stayed with Gramma for two weeks while Aunt Bea, my uncle, and their two children, Kathy and Jimmy, went to Florida on a vacation. Now that I look back, it truly was a blessing because as I kissed her good-bye, she said, "I will not be here when you get back." I smiled at her, assured her she would be, and gave her a big hug. My grandmother died the next month after falling down the stairs. God bless her. I felt love and sadness at her loss. It was if she had been able to say good-bye to us. I was deeply happy and fortunate that I had been able to have so much time with her during my life. She was a truly kind and loving grandmother.

CHAPTER 10

Yuma Test Station, Arizona

IN JANUARY 1957, we were on our way to Yuma, Arizona, in a brand-new Ford station wagon, which was very stylish with a gray-and-white exterior and a red-leather interior, and it was very roomy. Debbie was so good; after her bottle, I would lay her down in the backseat, all cozy with her blanket and stuffed animals. We made do with what we had available to tend to her needs. This kind of improvisation became part of my life as an army wife. Since there were only cloth diapers at the time, I asked our family for old towels to use for diapers. After rinsing them in a fabric softener, they were perfect. After changing Debbie on our trip west, I would toss them out at the gas stations' trash. Perfect!

I was so happy I had those makeshift diapers. We also boiled the rubber nipples from Debbie's milk bottles in an electric coffee pot at night in the motel. The rubber pants were washed and hung up on twine we brought with us.

This trip was very long, mostly across the vast state of Texas. As we drove, I saw landscapes that I never had seen before; I must say the rock formations were unbelievable. They were magnificent and huge, some towering hundreds of feet in the air. Others looked like boulders piled atop each other as if a giant child had been playing with them. Some had colors, mainly shades of brown and red streaking through them, as if an artist had painted a vast and beautiful landscape. These images were awe inspiring.

It was necessary, though, on this very long drive to keep Debbie entertained. Debbie loved me to read *The Three Little Kittens That Lost Their Mittens* over and over; no other story would do. By the time we reached Yuma, Bill was ready to burn that book. I am sure he knew the story by heart at that point.

We had gone from magnificent mountain vistas to the stark beauty of the desert. The land had become mostly flat and filled with brown hues and shades. Yuma was a flat desert town, with one main street with a few shops, wooden walkways, and wooden overhangs to protect the pedestrians mainly from the noonday sun. There were many trailer parks as well as Native Americans walking the street, wrapped in blankets and their traditional tall, black hats with a large brim. We had approximately twenty-five more miles before we would reach Yuma Test Station. The view was like a postcard: sand dunes, tall flowered cacti, and coal-black hills in the distance.

We were issued temporary quarters until our new quarters, along with many more, were finished. Every day Debbie and I would walk over and check out any progress. One evening the three of us drove into Yuma and purchased five rooms of furniture. We were fortunate enough to save money while Bill was in Korea. What a joy it was to move into a brand-new house with furniture delivered from the department store, plus an interior decorator that helped us arrange the furniture. This seemed like a once-in-a-lifetime experience!

Easter was approaching; I drove to Yuma and purchased a large chocolate bunny for Debbie and a few other items, naturally. I returned home to find the bunny had melted down to about an inch of chocolate in the box. I gave Debbie a spoon so she had a treat, and then the remaining chocolate went into the freezer. Luckily, Debbie did not care if the chocolate looked like a bunny or not. She simply loved the flavor.

This was an interesting learning experience; the morning was cool when I left, but it was ninety degrees when I returned at noon.

By the time I hung out a line of diapers, I could go right back where I started and take them down. Hot means *very hot* in Yuma and dry also.

My mom and dad flew out to visit. Never having been on a plane before, they were very excited and overwhelmed with the old western town of Yuma and the magnitude of the desert. The Indians walking the streets or sitting at the railroad station whittling their small wooden objects fascinated them. Even though I had written in detail about the brand-new housing out in "no man's land," it surprised them. They had expected to see the "Old West" complete with wooden homes and swinging doors on saloons. But they saw modern homes and no cowboys walking the streets at dawn waiting for a gunfight.

While they were with us, Bill drove us west to California. It was a big treat for Bill and me just to enjoy green trees. It's funny the things we missed when before we took them for granted, like trees and rain. They seem like such an ordinary part of life in the northeast where so much is green, with many streams, rivers, and lakes and plenty of rain and snow. When we were in Yuma, however, it seemed as if we had landed on an alien world with a completely barren landscape. So going into the mountains of California with the abundance of green trees was for us like a big ice cream sundae.

Going up and down through the mountains was exciting to us but not to my dad. He was very nervous, and even more so when he found out that we had to return this way. There was a narrow, two-way, winding road without a guardrail on one side, mountain on the other. As we looked down, the eighteen-wheeler trucks resembled matchbox toys. It took a long time for us to get to the bottom. I felt sorry for my dad because I could see he was a bit of a nervous wreck by the time we finally got there.

Then it was on to Disneyland. That was such a fun time for all of us but mostly for Debbie. She loved Mickey Mouse, who was the hit of the day. Also, the seals that barked delighted her. As she watched them, she laughed and clapped her little hands. And we smiled. Then on to Knotts' Berry Farm, a complete change from spotless Disney to dirt roads, a one-room schoolhouse, and a country store. It was truly the image of the Old West, and it was delightful. Altogether, this was a much needed and a perfect getaway.

Another day we drove south to Mexicalli, Mexico, over the border. As we approached a parking spot, small, very dirty six- to eight-year-old boys ran up to Bill with their hands out for money, promising to watch our car. Ha! They walked right along with us, begging for money. Bill finally gave the boys some change to get rid of them. I'm sure they knew that would work, and it did. It was a very strange feeling to see children begging. This was not a part of the world I was used to. It just doesn't seem right that children have to live like that anywhere.

The little border town was so disgustingly filthy that we didn't stay long. I had expected to see a place of beauty with friendly, happy people. I was not prepared to see the level of poverty and its concurrent lack of cleanliness that seemingly pervaded the entire place. Seeing freshly killed chickens, hanging by their feet and covered with flies, made my stomach turn. Also, merchants were yelling and begging us to buy their wares. They were very loud, aggressive, and frightening. I was very pleased when we all made the decision not to stay there any longer.

About now, Yuma Test Station looked more like a beachfront resort than it previously had, even if we had poisonous snakes and scorpions. This was paradise compared to Mexicali. The army supplied the grass seed so my dad was convinced he could get grass to grow in the desert, and he did, all right. He spent most of the mornings and evenings watering the sand. He met most of the neighbors, and that's how we met Diane and Ben Anderson (we still correspond). Debbie could not pronounce Mrs. Anderson; she said "Adza" and called Ben "Benny." Ben's not a Benny kind of guy, but he allowed it from her.

Once a month the army wives held a casual coffee to (greet and meet) the new wives. I was so happy to attend with my mother so she could meet my new friends. All the ladies loved to meet visiting families and friends. She was impressed by all the silver tea sets and trays. Many of the officers' wives had tours in Germany with their husbands and returned with tea sets, embroidered linens, and many other elegant items such as oil paintings. Mom really had a marvelous morning.

Before Mom and Dad went home, Mom made me a complete maternity wardrobe since I was expecting in September. I hated to see them leave, but they had to return home. At this point, I realized that life was a never-ending series of moves for us from place to place with friends and family coming to visit us wherever we might be. Home is not a place; home is people.

We got back to our day-by-day routine. Bill would leave for the airfield in the morning, and soon after, Debbie would wake up. We'd have our breakfast, put our bathing suits on, and walk over to the swimming pool. That was the best time to swim. Debbie played in the little kids' pool with all the other children. The ladies would take turns watching the little ones in the pool or baby carriages so the mothers could swim. We all kept in good shape and had beautiful tans.

Bill returned from work as we came back so we could have lunch together. It worked out perfectly. Bill would leave, and

Debbie had her bath and then was down for a nap. The days we didn't go for a swim, Debbie would play in the backyard, but first I would go out with a broom in order to move the sand around, looking for poisonous snakes, known as sidewinders, and scorpions. Thank God, I never found anything.

As I approached my due date, I was showing signs of a miscarriage, and I was ordered off my feet. We hired Suzie, our usual babysitter, a tiny Oriental lady married to a serviceman on post. Bill would get Debbie out of bed, change her diaper, and then leave for the airstrip. Suzie would appear, smiling as usual. Debbie was always happy to see Suzie. She would feed Debbie, bathe her, and of course, get her dressed. Debbie was such a quiet little girl and loved her dollhouse, swings, and books.

Suzie made the beds, cleaned up, and took Debbie for a walk before it got too hot. If we could keep the temperature down to eighty degrees in the house, it would be good. We had a large air conditioner and custom-made draperies throughout the house. The temperature did come down at night. Thank God.

I stayed off my feet most of the time. Bill and I drove into Yuma for my doctor's appointment, and the doctor's orders were to "go to a store and buy a toothbrush and anything else you will need; you're going to have this baby today. Check into the hospital, and I will be there to meet you at five o'clock." We did what he ordered, and when he arrived, the doctor induced labor. Bill missed Debbie's birth so this was his first experience with my labor pains. He was with me all the time, playing the game "dots" to pass the time until I was rolled into the delivery room. Fathers were not allowed in at that time.

Finally, on September 25, 1957, a healthy, eight-pound baby boy, William J. Gorman Jr., came into the world. Later the doctor came into my room and picked up the white box that held Bill's baby book. As he talked to me, he also drew a circle representing a baby and then a line going to a smaller circle symbolizing a twin! I had no idea I had conceived twins. This news was shocking, but if I'd known I was expecting twins, it would have been disastrous. I was prepared for one, not two infants. But as always in life, I learned to handle what I had to.

As Bill grew up, he had the energy of two healthy kids; he was never bad, just a rascal. He'd pull the bow on my apron so it fell to the floor or unplug the vacuum cleaner while it was being used. I sometimes wonder what if there were "two little Bills." Oh heavens!

The Yuma Test Station was a fascinating place. Not only were there, of course, helicopters, airplanes and soldiers, but also many military objects were buried in the sand to test their longevity. It seemed like the world's biggest time capsule that was meant to be opened only by those with special clearances.

One place that I thought to be particularly clever was the beauty parlor named the "Test Curl." If you can have test planes and pilots, why not test haircutters and hairdos?

One of Bill's duties at the test base was flying a group of army paratroopers, probably from the 101st Airborne Division, out to the desert to practice jumping out of a moving helicopter safely.

Just about every Sunday night, the phone would ring, and some hiker or hikers were lost or hurt in the desert's rugged and very difficult terrain. Bill would fly over the desert for hours until they were found. There were neither cell phones nor GPSs then! It was a relief when Howard (Toady) Phillipps, a helicopter pilot, and his wife Jean were assigned to the airfield. He and Bill took turns taking the distress calls on Sunday evenings. We became very good friends.

One day my neighbor, Irene, came over to visit with her daughter, Diane. She was a very active little girl. Debbie and Diane were about three years old and played together most of the time. Irene and I sat in the living room while the girls played in Debbie's room. After a while, we checked on the girls. We were shocked to find the girls with big, fat crayons in their hands. They had scribbled all over the white walls with red and green colors!

Ordinarily in the civilian world, this would not be a big deal. Young children are prone to do this sort of thing. In the military world though, things are different. Now came the big problem— how to remove the colorful artwork. No one had an answer. We finally had to sneak a painter in the house at night in order to paint the room. The army did not allow service personnel to paint the walls, cabinets, or other spaces in the quarters. After that surprise, all crayons were off limits unless I supervised the event.

This place seemed to be full of surprises. During the summer months, a vegetable truck would slowly go through the neighborhood. When I heard the horn, I would run out, holding my apron out so the driver would give me free honeydew melons or maybe grapefruit. Next time he'd have vegetables. We never knew, but we didn't care. It was free and a pleasant surprise. We never really knew why the driver gave away the free produce, but it was like a gift on a very hot Christmas.

Even the weather there could play tricks on us and cause the unexpected. We were having our usual sunny day when a large black cloud came over the test station. Of course, I thought this must be a large rainstorm coming, but I was wrong. It was not rain, not a thunderstorm, but thousands of crickets! A deafening sound erupted, plus a wave of crickets seemed to crash over us like a large wave coming in at the seashore covering everything in sight. I took the garden hose and washed the front of the house, but they would quickly return. I figured they probably liked the cool, wet house so I discontinued the operation. One managed to find a way into our air conditioner; we lost some sleep over that nonstop racket. The crickets seemed to be like something out of an ancient biblical plague. They never seemed to stop.

Driving was hazardous—stepping on the brakes was like driving on ice since the crickets made it so slippery. That wasn't the worst of it. When they finally died, the odor was so pungent that it was sickening. We cleaned up the remains by the shovelful—a nasty job, something I never wanted to do again. I shudder whenever I think about it.

Young Bill was about eighteen months old when I said to Bill, "I'd like to have another baby, but I do not want to carry a child through the summer." Bill thought it was fine and was happy with that plan. He was so thoughtful, getting up during the night and always taking the four o'clock feeding with young Bill. Bill always did his part and more.

It was Christmas, and Bill had a massive boil on the very end of his spine. This was definitely the worst time of year for such a problem. The doctor wanted him to go to the Los Angeles hospital, but he would not go and be away for Christmas. He could not sit or walk, and he was in severe pain. Our friends, Cynthia and Raymond Powell, came over to help trim the Christmas tree. Bill was lying on the couch flat on his stomach while pointing out to us where every ornament should be placed. Since Cynthia was Jewish and never had a Christmas tree, the evening was most enjoyable. We all laughed most of the time, even though I could see Bill sometimes wincing in pain from the laughing.

I left that silly group in order to attend midnight Mass in a chapel just around the corner; the Powells kept Bill company. Upon my return, I fixed the traditional Christmas breakfast. Soon after, reality set in as to how tired we all were. Cynthia and Raymond didn't have children, but Bill and I had to be up for Debbie and

53

Bill in a few hours. Without a doubt, that was the happiest, most fun-filled Christmas I ever had.

Living in the desert, cabin fever sets in; so the post commander's wife, Carrie Baker, had an outstanding idea to keep us occupied. She provided an Old West show for the officers' wives to produce with some of their husbands. The show called for can-can dancers, including me. I had to let out the news that I was pregnant. Oh well! So Carrie remarked, "Don't worry, you can be the wayward woman in the show." (So how about that!)

Show time!

We were not on a stage, so the audience was on the same level as us. That was perfect because they became part of the show. The setting was an Old West barroom with joke telling, people moving about, and much laughter. Ben was the bartender plus part of the quartet. Surprisingly, they harmonized like professionals. We had hidden talent on post. Ginny Rainscuk made all the dresses and did a wonderful job. Diane, Jean, and several girls wore these bright-colored creations including many petticoats and danced in the fashionable can-can manner. They were a big hit. Then there was the usual sheriff in town, making trouble and bickering with the cowboys. Over in a dimly lit corner sat the wayward woman, wearing a long, black dress and a large brimmed hat that partially covered my face. All the while, I'm weeping, holding a long handkerchief and letting it flow from hand to hand and occasionally touching the corners of my eyes. The cast talked among themselves about how ashamed I should be, and the audience chimed in. I had a hard time not smiling and laughing during the whole thing. After all, I was supposed to be "the fallen woman." Actually, the whole event was so much fun that it was uplifting. The evening was a success, and everyone had a smile on his or her face after the club closed for the night.

It was entirely too hot in the afternoon to go outdoors. We would venture out after dinner so Debbie could ride her tricycle, take a walk, and visit the neighbors. I would mess around with my flowers, but I had to watch for any scorpions. I did not want to be stung, and I had to watch out for Debbie also. That would have been even worse.

While potentially dangerous, it was also such an interesting place. There were things there that I would never have seen back east. For example, we all used petrified wood that resembled marble with different shades of brown and was very heavy to make a border around the flowerbeds. We were sorry we didn't bring some home with us back east for fun and a perfect conversation starter. It was so specific to that area—hot, dry, dangerous, beautiful, surprising, and unusual.

My due date was rapidly approaching, so my mother flew out a few weeks before the expected delivery. Naturally, I was extremely relieved that she would be there to help care for Debbie and Bill. (little Bill, only a year and a half old, pronounced his name "Bull.") She was a true godsend, helping with just about anything she could, from babysitting, to shopping and cleaning, to just talking with me. I was so appreciative for her help, especially because I knew the level of pain she was experiencing. My mother had severe pain from arthritis in her hands and arm joints, but by the time she went home, she could hold a comb in order to comb the back of her hair. The combination of the Arizona heat and dry air along with the constantly using her joints to help me did the trick and relieved some of her pain.

On Sunday night, March 22, 1959, my labor pains began. So off Bill and I went to the *old* Yuma hospital where Bull was born because the *new* hospital, supposedly much improved, was in the process of moving that day to the new Parkview Hospital. We didn't know the exact location, and both Bill and I were starting to worry. We hoped the delivery would not be the kind that you read about in the newspapers—"Husband delivers wife's baby in backseat of car." Luckily, Bill noticed a patrol car parked at a gas station, so he asked for directions. We were surprised by a police escort with flashing lights! It was such a relief and exciting also. How often does a person get a police escort somewhere?

As I was wheeled into my room, the nurses were making up the beds and tearing plastic covering from new blankets. Bill joined me soon after, and the labor pains lessened. The next thing I realized, I was waking up and still pregnant, with no new baby in our lives. Bill was still sitting there waiting. He was pretending to be patient and calm. As always, he was there for me.

"It'll be fine, Doll. Don't worry," he said and smiled.

I knew it would be as long as we had each other.

Then the doctor induced labor, and in time, six-pound Linda Mary was born at 3:12 p.m. She was so tiny with dark-brown, curly hair and a round face, like a baby doll. She was such a content baby as long as she had her thumb in her mouth.

Debbie was very excited to have a baby sister, but Bull was not interested. All he needed were his trucks. Linda had a milk allergy and drank soymilk, brown in color with an offensive odor. Plus, her little body was 50 percent covered with an itchy rash. Most of her childhood, she smelled like Desitin cream, which eased the discomfort.

The neighbors stopped in one evening to see baby Linda, and after they left, a big scorpion ran across the living room floor headed for the couch where my mother and I were sitting. My mother and I saw it and froze. But Bill quickly stomped on it, and we relaxed. From then on, we covered the bassinet with netting.

We never saw anymore but stayed on the lookout for them. A scorpion resembles a small, brown lobster with eight legs, carries its tail with a venomous stinger over its body, and moves with great speed. They are poisonous—life threatening to small children and dangerous to everyone else. So we were not going to take any chances at all with our children.

This locale continued to be full of surprises, many of them meteorological. Most days were bright and full of sunshine except for an occasional flash flood. At times, these sudden deluges were very dangerous. The rain from miles away would run down into the desert with great force. One storm made a large ditch next to our quarters, continued down into the back doors of some quarters, and out the front doors, ruining furniture, rugs, and everything in its path. The power of that storm and flood was awful. It made me think that despite all of our knowledge, humanity is very small in the face of nature and God. We were very lucky that the flood missed us—very lucky indeed!

It took a lot of cleanup and painting for the quarters to be livable again. It would have been an enormous task to rebuild. More importantly, though, no one was hurt. Thank God. I understand completely that things are replaceable, but people are not.

There always seemed to be some kind of adventures going on in the desert. Since we lived so far away from any stores, I always kept a small pickle jar under the front seat of the car. Preparation was something that I learned as an army wife. If young Bill had to urinate, this jar came in handy.

One day while driving for a while, young Bill naturally had to "pee pee" as he said. He was sitting between Bill and me in a car seat, and he was very anxious. I quickly located the jar from under the seat and aimed it at him, and he began to relieve himself. But I had misjudged the direction a bit and the amount he had to urinate. As the jar started filling, I kept saying, "Stop, Bill, stop!"

As Bill was trying to find a place to pull over, the urine began to run down young Bill's legs and socks and into his shoes as well as on my hands and arm, the car seat, and the car itself. Bill was trying hard to focus on driving and pulling over, but he broke out into laughter. Laughing, he pulled over while Debbie, in the backseat, was giggling away. I had nothing but paper napkins to clean us up with, and the aroma in the hot Yuma day was overwhelming. At the time, I didn't think this was funny, but soon after, I did. When the kids talk about it now, we all laugh, even young Bill.

Toady – Yuma Test Station

Bill flying at Armed Forces Day – Yuma Test Station

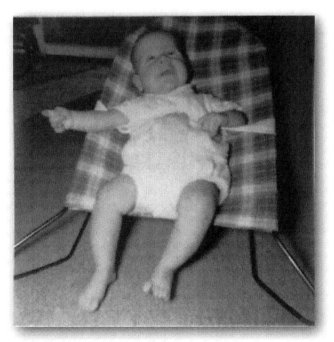

William J. Gorman, Jr.

Linda Mary Gorman

CHAPTER 11

Arizona

HERE WE WERE headed for New Jersey, just a pleasure trip, mainly for the family to see the kids. It was a very nice, although a very short, visit. We loved seeing the family, and they loved seeing the kids. I was sad that we had to leave right away. Much to our surprise, Bill's parents decided to make the trip back to Arizona with us. What an adventure that was!

For our cross-country trip, I decided right away to bring along a much larger pickle jar. No use in taking any chances! We also had a small, bright-yellow children's toilet, which was a perfect replica of a standard toilet, for the girls. We were hesitant to take them into service stations' restrooms since they were usually filthy. Thank goodness, that has changed for the better with the times.

The luggage was strapped to the top of the station wagon, with seven of us inside the car. It was like a sight from a Chevy Chase movie. Bill concocted a makeshift table that clamped on the back of the middle seat, even with cup holders for the kids. It was perfect for eating, drawing, and playing games. Also in the back was Linda in her bouncy chair with her thumb in her mouth. She was a happy baby. Everything worked well with the air mattresses, pillows, and blankets. The kids loved it. They were happy and traveled very well, which made the rest of us happy as well.

I would hop over the seat and make peanut-butter sandwiches for the kids. We always had a cooler for milk, water, and lunchmeat.

We stopped at about four o' clock after we found a motel with a restaurant and better yet, a swimming pool. That made everyone happy and gave the kids a chance to burn off some energy and for Bill and me to exercise.

In Texas, Ella could not believe the massive rock formations were not made by people. Some looked as if they were sculptures made by a giant, with loops or rock stretching into the air and delicately balanced. While they are very heavy, some looked as if a slight wind would knock them over. But they endure. Ella was in awe of their unusual and staggering beauty.

They also noticed that in the land of the Old West, with all those hundreds of miles of bare land, there was not a single sign of a cowboy! Just where were the Texas Rangers, the Lone Ranger, or even John Wayne?

While Ella and Hen were with us in Yuma, Bill made captain (two silver bars). This invitation went out to all officers and wives for Bill's "wetting down," the slang for celebration of promotion.

> I thought my name was lost in the
> Archives of the Pentagon but they
> Found it! I'm not a lieutenant any longer,
> But a Captain! You are invited to join me
> In "wetting them down" at the Officers'
> Open Mess on Tuesday, 10 November 1959
> From 1700 to 1900 hours.
>
> WILLIAM J. GORMAN
> CAPTAIN, INF

The Officers' Club supplied a large buffet and an "open bar"; so naturally, we all did an excellent job of celebrating. Bill's parents had never seen that many officers in their uniforms and their ladies in lovely cocktail dresses. They were very impressive!

While they were with us, Bill was assigned larger quarters. That made us happy, but it was the most confusing move we made, and it was only one block away. It seemed as if it should have been easy, but with so many people, we kept getting in each other's way. Again, it seemed like a scene from a goofy comedy movie. If we only had fast-food takeout, it would have been easy. But such things did not exist there. Feeding a family and moving was not easy. Ella and Henry were used to three meals a day at eight, twelve, and five o'clock; I could not serve peanut-butter sandwiches! They were very understanding people, but they were older and a bit set in their ways. Regardless of the running around, we made all the meals and moved all of our stuff. It all worked out eventually, but Bill and I were frazzled!

Ella and Henry stayed for Christmas, and we all enjoyed the kids. We had Jean and Toady over for dinner. I was happy Ella and Henry got to know some of our friends. Ella just loved listening to Toady with his southern accent. We had a very happy Christmas, plus watching Toady and Jean play with toys was fun (they were like kids). It was an outstanding day!

Ella and Henry left soon after the holiday, so we got back to our day-to-day routine. We had been stationed in Yuma Test Station for three and a half years when we finally received orders for Germany. We were thrilled, me most of all. Leaving Yuma, Bill had orders for Fort Benning, Georgia, which was estimated to be about a three-month assignment, and then on to Germany.

This took some planning! First on the "to-do list" were shots, even another vaccination. Surviving the "hurt in arm," as the kids would say, we all did very well. In order to drive off the post, we were obligated to have a clearance noting we had no debts on post. This was no problem; we were free and clear. My big job was packing clothes for everyone, starting with travel clothes from Yuma to Georgia, plus Bill's uniforms to wear at Fort Benning. There was one TDY shipment (temporary duty) going to Fort Benning, ironing board, iron, toys, TV, any warm clothes for traveling to Germany, plus more uniforms for Bill.

Going in storage for three years were the living-room set, dining-room set, washer, dryer, refrigerator, three bedroom sets, kitchen table and chairs, rugs, and more. That was all packed in very large wooden crates. There was so much to do in preparation, but Bill and I worked it out, as we always did.

For Germany, the moving company packed everything in large boxes. Packers packed everything and anything, even trash. It sounds funny, but it has happened. Servicemen's wives figured out some tricks of their own. For instance, I had a large dried-flower arrangement, so I hung it inside my portable dishwasher. Another friend pinned a large, starched, lace table doily to the inside roof of the car. Also, I put coffee grains in a stocking and placed them in a refrigerator or freezer. Charcoal works too in helping stop odor and mildew when being stored.

Then came the time for cleaning our quarters! Army regulations stated there would be no enhancements or disfigurements of the quarters, interior or exterior. That meant no holes in the wall. Well, of course, we all hung pictures. I don't know anyone who has not wanted to decorate or put his or her own personal touches on living spaces, but then we had to deal with fixing any holes that might have been left. This, however, was no problem. We simply filled the holes with white toothpaste. We cleaned the bedrooms as the packers finished, but the kitchen was difficult.

We needed to clean but also to eat. Living out in the desert, there were no fast-food places available. Thankfully, several of our friends who were still stationed there had us over for dinner.

That was a blessing. As I mentioned before, everything had to be spotless; Bill and I spent hours cleaning the stove, mostly the oven, with steel cleaning pads. No spray oven cleaner existed then. You never knew if the inspector would run his "white gloved" hand inside the oven. This made me very nervous. The process was certainly intimidating, but we passed. No problem. Amen!

We were wined and dined in fashion. The Andersons left before us; Jean and Toady were leaving with us and joining us at Fort Benning. It was sad leaving our other friends, but we were looking forward to seeing mountains, most of all Germany, and naturally, the families.

CHAPTER 12

———— ✿ ————

Fort Benning, Georgia

WE WERE TRAVELING to Fort Benning, Georgia, for a three-month tour en route to Germany. Driving along, we went through a rain shower. Debbie asked, "What are those black things people have over their head?" They were umbrellas. It was something the children had not seen before, and I realized that there would be so many new things for them to see and learn about. The very few times it rained in Yuma, we would all go out and jump in the puddles. That was always so much fun. They wanted to do it now, but we had to keep dry so they would be fine when we got there.

Upon arriving at Fort Benning, we were lucky to find an apartment; these were usually available to army personnel only for short terms. Everything was going along very well until Bill came home with some news. This is what he said: "Since the Berlin wall went up, no more dependents can go to Germany." What a shock. The kids and I would have to stay back in the states I thought. I was numb and so disappointed that I just stared at him. Then he said, "But, Doll, I know where I can buy you a fur coat cheap. We have a choice between Alaska and France. Where do you want to go?"

This was just too much for me to process! It took a few seconds to understand what he just said. Then I understood what he had told me. It wasn't at all about a present to make me feel better, but the family would stay together! Then I stood up, threw my arms around his neck, and just held on. I was so thankful we would all be together. When I gathered my thoughts, we conferred with each other about the options, but it didn't really take long. We decided Alaska would be the safest place for all of us. Everything went very well in Georgia, so before we knew it, we were on to Jersey.

When we arrived at Bill's parents' house in New Jersey, a telegram was waiting for Bill from the army stating, "Stay in New Jersey until further notice." Our thoughts were "Now what?" The second telegram arrived a few days later. It stated, "Proceed to Fort Sill, Oklahoma, for Instrument Training School en route to Alaska." In order to survive in snowy Alaska, a pilot finds it difficult to determine the difference between snow-covered mountains and the sky, referred to as "white out"; so it was necessary for any new pilot going to Alaska to learn a completely new set of techniques and information when flying by instruments only.

So here we were in New Jersey, particularly with only the clothes on our backs! Once again, we had to improvise for temporary necessities. I put out the word to all family and friends for old towels, iron, pots, and pans, keeping in mind that everything had to be squeezed into the car and that they must be items no longer needed. These items would be trashed upon leaving Fort Sill since only personal luggage was allowed on the ship to Alaska. Our empty car, except for a child's car seat, went with us.

By now, Debbie was six years old, Bill four, and Linda two, and we had to say our "good-byes" to our family and friends. It was most difficult for our parents, knowing they would not see their grandchildren for three years. Saying "good-bye" to my dear Aunt Bea, my mother's baby sister, was heart breaking. She was in the hospital, dying of cancer. That was a very sad day. I really don't know how I got through it, knowing I would never see her again. She died two months later. I loved her throughout my life, and I would continue to love her after her death.

CHAPTER 13

Fort Sill, Oklahoma

AFTER A LONG, hot trip across country without air conditioning, we were beat! The journey took several days. As we journeyed through Oklahoma, the territory grew very hot and very dry. Long stretches of farmland, with grains growing against a backdrop of wide sky, went on for miles. We also saw rock formations by the edge of the desert that, like in Texas, were beautiful but stark and colored through in reddish tones.

Even though the kids were very good travelers, they were cranky and tired by the time we arrived. As was the case so many times, we had to find housing for ourselves. While some housing is available on bases, it is often on a first-come, first-served basis, and frequently, there simply isn't enough to go around. Each family had to add their names to a waiting list and hope for the best. Fortunately for us, we were experienced home hunters, and we set to work on our mission immediately.

Right to a realtor we went, and luckily, we were able to rent a furnished three-bedroom house with a washer and dryer. Perfect!

The next thing we had to consider was supplies for our temporary home. We had to stop at the commissary for milk, bread, snacks, paper goods, and the rest of any household necessities that I could think of. I bought an initial amount of supplies, but then I did a much more thorough shopping trip later. Bill and the kids waited in the car as I shopped. Surprisingly, I walked right into Rip and Jerry Collins, friends from flight school. When I came out of the commy with them behind me, Bill was shocked. I was happy for Bill; this way Rip could show him the "lay of the land" on post.

In setting up house, the handed-down items from home really helped. It was a challenge because we had to keep what we had to a minimum. So with the few pots, pans, and utensils I had to work with, it was more like camping out. The kids were very good about it because I always made the situation into an adventure for them if I could.

Bill was very busy with his training. He was up early, went to class every day, and was home at night. Even though he had so much to learn, he was always a family man and would be with us whenever he could.

We also had our share of entertainment. Rip and Jerry took all of us fishing in the nearby lake, which was very beautiful. For the adults, this was a chance to have a change of scenery and relax, and for the kids, it was very exciting, especially if they caught a little sunfish.

We also had a few dinners out with Rip and Jerry. Having good friends there was an enormous boon to us. We enjoyed the food and drink, of course, but spending time with people we knew and cared about was far more important. This social inter-action is crucial and important for families to develop if they have the often-nomadic lives that those in the military do.

The weather was unpredictable and difficult. It was frequently windy. When the gusts blew like a giant trying to knock down a toy town, attempting to hang sheets outside was impossible; they wrapped right around the clothesline. Unfortunately, that meant that the children often had to stay inside. When the winds were bad, the dirt would kick up, and it could easily get in their eyes and noses. So they watched the *I Love Lucy* TV show most of the time since they didn't like the little red ants that would bite them when the critters got into their summer shorts.

Unfortunately, it was tornado season, a time of great worry for everyone. This area is part of the swath of land in the United States called Tornado Alley. It runs from Texas and Oklahoma through parts of the northern area of the Midwest. This area of the country typically sees more tornados than everywhere else does. People were used to expecting the terrible storms and preparing for them.

Therefore, on TV a scope ran across the screen showing where the heavy rain appeared and where locations of possible tornados were. This news made me sooo nervous! I was always wondering if a twister was going to come our way, but not one ever appeared. We did experience one big storm with large hailstones and pounding torrential rain. At one point, I worried that the windowpanes would crack, plus the overwhelming noise sounded like what I thought cannon fire might be! It was a scary night. But it was not a tornado.

Bill finished the course he was attending, came home, and packed the car, and we were off to Oakland, California. Diane and Ben were stationed there, and that's where the ship docked in order to take us to Alaska. Finally!

CHAPTER 14

California

AFTER DIANE AND Ben left Yuma, they were stationed at Fort Holabirth, Maryland, with the army intelligence program. Later, Ben changed his branch of service from ordnance to what currently is the military intelligence branch. He was then stationed at Oakland, attending army language school, and then on to Honduras.

Once they knew we would be in Oakland, they insisted we stay in their quarters instead of the military guesthouse. Looking out of their living-room window, we could see the harbor and the USS *General W. A. Mann*, a huge navy transport vessel, the same ship that took Bill to Korea and would take us to Alaska. Diane and Ben were the best. They were really superb hosts, driving us to all the interesting points in the San Francisco area. They showed us the remarkable streets of San Francisco with their twists and turns and incredible rises and falls, including some that were so steep that cable cars were the preferred method of going up and down them. Ben drove us up and down such steep, narrow, and curving roads. It was certainly scary and felt a bit like a slow-motion roller coaster, but I loved it. Thank goodness, Ben knew the roads and was an excellent driver.

One of the trips Ben and Diane took us on was to the redwood forests. The colossal redwoods were unbelievable; it is amazing that trees could possibly grow to that proportion. Even though they are living things, these trees seemed more like skyscrapers in the concrete canyons in Manhattan than part of a magnificent and ancient forest three thousand miles away from New York City.

Our last night there, we had a babysitter for the evening, and we "went out on the town." It was good to be able to have adult time. I always thought that New York City was the place of giant human structures, but San Francisco has some claims to this achievement. The Golden Gate Bridge is like something out of a fairy tale. During the day, it is a stunning sight as the span stretches seemingly forever. Driving over the Golden Gate Bridge at night, however, made it seem magical. With the thousands of lights against its deep color, it sparkled like diamonds high against the dark sky. It looked like an army of fairies holding flames illuminating the bridge. The Golden Gate Bridge looked like a gorgeous painting done by a huge, celestial artist. It was truly sublime and awe inspiring.

We had dinner at the House of Prime Rib on Van Ness Avenue. This was more than simply a steakhouse. It is one of the oldest and finest restaurants in San Francisco. The building, both the outside and the internal décor, is exquisite. It looks like something out of a Victorian British painting, with deep wood tones. The prime rib was carved and served individually at our table from a silver, heated cart. There were also potatoes, a vegetable, and Yorkshire pudding. This was the finest of British cuisine, and it was simply scrumptious. The wine was excellent, and even the rolls were delicious. It was a wonderful meal.

Then dessert was served; a silver teacart appeared carrying examples of whatever fancied your palate. They were picture perfect and excellently presented; unfortunately, we restrained ourselves and settled for coffee. I wish I could have eaten something, but I was completely full. It was an extraordinary dinner, and one I will always remember. I'd like to go back someday.

From there we went to the Fairmount Hotel on Nob Hill where a slow-moving merry-go-round was the cocktail lounge. As we sat at a small table to have a drink, it would slowly go around. It was as if we had stepped back in time to the very early twentieth century around 1910. As we sat there, we felt the pace of time slow, as if we were in the past. It was a wonderful way to enjoy a drink and relax.

The next pleasure was right across the street, The Top of the Mark Hotel. We rode the elevator to the top. The door opened into a large dining room encircled in glass. The view was breathtaking. Drinks or dinner was available, but we didn't have either. Instead, we simply walked around and enjoyed the spectacular view of San Francisco. Next, we caught the cable car near Lombard Street. That was fun, watching people jump on or off as they pleased. We rode down a huge hill to the turntable at the bottom of the hill and then into the Buena Vista Tavern, famous for its Irish coffee concoction. There was a large crowd there, standing room only. The coffee (very strong and topped with whipped cream) was served in a large glass. After that, we went back to the foot of Hyde Street where the cable car turntable was, and everyone, really only the men, helped the brakeman turn the arriving car around. We got on and had a ride back up the hill. It was such fun! We returned to Ben's parked car and proceeded back over the bridge. I will always fondly treasure the memory of this wonderful evening.

Alaska—here we come!

CHAPTER 15

On the Way to Alaska

Early in the morning, Ben drove us to the pier in order to board the ship, the USS *Mann*. We were so excited about finally being on our way to Alaska. We thought this trip would be relaxing, our newest adventure! As we climbed up the gangplank, we heard this announcement over the loudspeaker: "Captain Gorman, report to the commander." This meant Bill would be on duty for the entire trip. He left us standing on the deck, watching all the military families boarding. A small band played "The Star Spangled Banner," "God Bless America," and other patriotic songs. The tears rolled down my cheeks; it was very moving. I now have an inkling how our troops must feel leaving the United States when going to war.

Once again over the loudspeaker, another announcement: "The female dependent with small children [that meant me] on deck, take cover," meaning that the children and I needed to go inside the ship. I guess he thought the kids would fall overboard, but they would not leave my side. With head down, I felt like a bad little girl being sent to her room. It was embarrassing that I had been singled out as someone who might be in danger.

As we sailed out of Oakland, above us stood the incredible Golden Gate Bridge. I had seen this magnificent bridge from driving on it and from standing on the hills of San Francisco, and those views were amazing. Just last night we had driven over it, admiring the view of San Francisco. But to see it from below truly made me feel its majesty and power. From this angle, I could see the huge cables holding the bridge in place, stretching along and up the structure. Its color gleamed in the sunlight, casting a beautiful orange glow onto the water.

Then, on the left, there was another quintessential image of San Francisco but from a darker perspective than the rest of this beautiful city: Alcatraz prison. Looking at that large building, a completely different feeling came over me. I was depressed and squeamish, remembering some of the unbelievable stories told about that prison. It is a huge compound sitting alone on an island in the wild water of the San Francisco Bay. Its large buildings fill the island and seem to be built to withstand some kind of a siege by invading forces, but in reality, it was constructed to hold men. What a contrast that was, to move from the positive beauty of the Golden Gate Bridge to the negative, imposing power of that enormous jail.

As we started up the coast, a heavy fog rolled in. What I thought of as fog on the East Coast would only be the barest wisp of cloud here. Bill and I thought we would walk out on the deck and have a romantic moment. As Bill opened the door, we met a wall of fog, as if the entire ship was being swallowed by an enormous cloud that had descended from the heavens. Let's just say it provided the privacy for a brief but very romantic kiss. Then we had to go back inside.

Luckily for the kids and us, the ship had a large playroom for all the children. Finally, they had a chance to move around. There were swings, seesaws, toys, and cartoon movies. Debbie was so happy to see *Peter Pan* and *Snow White*. The kids loved it.

There was also onboard entertainment for the adults; we had movies or bingo in the evening and a small library. We were fortunate to be assigned a large cabin for the five of us. The kids particularly liked the bunk beds. If you wanted to dry anything from rubber baby pants (no plastic then) or your hair, the boiler room was the perfect place. Looking at a group of ladies with their hair in curlers and sitting under a line of baby pants was some sight. It was a one-time event. I wish I had had a camera!

At every meal, each family had their own young man as their server. He was a great help to me as Bill had to work, and I was seasick every morning. For those who have never experienced seasickness, it is like being on a roller coaster that keeps changing direction as it goes up and down and round and round, all the while riding it having eaten far too much junk food. The kids were good, but it was comforting to have someone looking over them.

On the last day, the captain of the ship gave the children a party with hats and balloons and serving ice cream and cake. The crew went out of their way to make everything enjoyable. We had a fabulous dinner that night with shrimp appetizers, steak, and the works, even candlelight! It was a pleasant ending to our trip.

When it was quiet at night, lying in a bunk bed, we could feel the movement of the ship and hear the low tones of the foghorn. It was both eerie and soothing. In the morning, the fog lifted, and we saw land: Alaska! July 1961. Where we docked, there was nothing but wide-open fields, not even a building.

USS Mann – North to Alaska

Ft. Richardson - Housing

CHAPTER 16

Fort Richardson, Alaska

OUR SPONSORS, CAPTAIN Bob Rose and his wife, Nell, were at the dock to meet us and answered many of our questions. We had never met them before, but we found them warm and caring. They had three little girls and a newborn baby boy. We quickly became good friends.

Anchorage was a bit of a distance away, not really far in terms of miles, but it seemed almost forever with the dusty roads and the lack of snow (except on the mountaintops) since it was summertime. It was like driving through untamed wilderness. As we approached Fort Richardson, the scenery improved, with tall pines and bright flowers.

Dinner at the Roses' quarters gave us an idea of how our quarters would be on post, but Anchorage would not be our home for a few months. Captain Rose drove us back to Anchorage where we would spend the night. This was an eye opener! I had expected something like the kind of place available in almost any city of a reasonable size in the lower forty-eight states. I was in for a surprise though. Alaska was a very different place. We stayed in a very old hotel, which was really a rooming house, on the ground floor. We were all in one large room, with only one bathroom down the hall. The startling part was our bed was right next to the window. Since it was a hot summer night, the window had to be opened. Bill could have put his hands out and touched any passerby.

There were many barrooms that produced people walking the streets, singing, laughing, and loudly talking. Any one of them could have fallen into our window. Even though it was late at night, it was still bright outside. This made both of us very nervous, and we could not relax enough to sleep. It made for a long night. This was the time of the extended day in Alaska. In the summer in Anchorage, its stays light until past midnight, hence the name the Land of the Midnight Sun. It seemed that some days, especially during the days nearest the summer solstice, were about twenty-two to twenty-three hours. This extended sunshine took a lot of getting used to and wreaked havoc on our sleeping schedules.

Since we arrived in Alaska during the summer, the sun would shine most of the time; even if you could not physically see it, the sky would be bright. Sleeping was a problem. We would lose track of time. All of a sudden, we would realize the kids were still playing outside at ten o'clock. Most newcomers had the same problem.

May, June, and July were the brightest months, and June 21 is the longest day because the sun does not set. There were many activities and parties to celebrate the coming summertime. The challenge was to stay awake!

Early the next morning, Bob came for us. I spent the morning with Nell and the kids. I don't know how she handled three little girls plus a newborn and then the five of us! Meanwhile, the men drove back to the pier in order to retrieve our car. That night we spent in the guesthouse. After last night, we were all exhausted.

We checked into Martin Arms, our future home for a few months. It was a large apartment complex. We rented a two-bedroom, first-floor apartment; it wasn't elaborate, truly a bare-bones sort of place, but it was a step up from the place we had been in.

Debbie started first grade in the Anchorage school system; I hated watching her get in the bus and having no idea where she was going. She was, however, a proud and brave little girl. Fortunately, other neighborhood children joined her. I think it bothered me a great deal more than it did her. For the kids, this was another adventure.

When we soon received our household shipment, it was like Christmas opening the boxes. I was happy to get the supplies and clothes we needed, but for the kids, they laughed with happiness in finding their toys and books.

Bill enjoyed flying up there and was with a good bunch of pilots. Every night he'd tell me how the mountains were so picturesque with the sun shining on the snow as he flew over them.

He loved to talk of their size and majesty, saying they were bigger, more beautiful, more majestic, and snowier—even in the summer—than any others he had ever seen. I loved listening to his descriptions of what he saw when he was flying. "Doll, I wish I could take you with me so you could see them yourself," he said and kissed me.

Bill had warned me that one Saturday night we would have a surprise visit from a few pilots and their wives because they wanted to meet us and check us out! It happened that we were sleeping when the knock came on the door. In walked Rosealie and Buel Powell, Dora and Wendall Thurman, and Joy and Glen Hickenbottom. Bill made coffee while I got out some Danish rolls. We had a good time, not knowing each other but talking and laughing as if we had been lifelong friends. I have always been delighted with the way the other families in the military have often gone out of their way to make newcomers feel welcome to what could sometimes be intimidating new environments.

The Officers' Club was our next meeting place, and it was a good-looking club too. The group was there before us, sitting at a table for eight. We made small talk at first; then all of a sudden, the ladies took off their high-heel shoes and proceeded to bang them on the tabletop! At the same time, they were yelling, "We want service," over and over again. Bill and I exchanged glances in disbelief! After a while, we figured this was all arranged with the bartender! They were always out for a laugh and good time, and they never failed. This happy bunch turned out to be our best friends with many laughs and merriment.

Of course, in addition to making new friends, we also had to equip our place with a variety of necessities. A large upright electric freezer was our first purchase. The apartment freezer in the refrigerator was just too small. My family back in New Jersey thought that was the funniest things anyone could do. "Buy a freezer while living in Alaska!"

Fortunately, we did not have to stay in the little apartment very long. What a happy day it was when we moved on post, 517 Apartment G, Seventh Street, in November, the perfect time before Christmas. Bill hung blinking colored Christmas lights across the front porch. We had the best show watching a female moose with her twin calves; there they stood mesmerized by the lights. The Eskimos in town did the same thing, watching the one and only traffic light we had change colors. I think we must have seemed like aliens to the animals and native peoples. We were truly strangers in a strange land.

We were pleased with the post housing. The first floor had a galley kitchen, dining area, and living room. Upstairs were three bedrooms and a bathroom. There was also a full basement, warm and dry, with a washer and plenty of room for toys of all sorts. The post housing also supplied slipcovers of different colors for the living-room furniture. What a good deal it was! Compared to the first boarding-room-like place and then the little apartment, this felt as if we had moved into a spacious old home.

This housing worked very well for us, especially because of the season. It was good to be able to have more rooms to use because now the extended darkness had set in, the exact opposite of the Land of the Midnight Sun; it could be named the Land of the Morning Darkness. In the winter, vehicles had to be plugged into an electric current or the motor would freeze. Whenever one was knocked out, mostly by a moose, there would be a problem! All you could do was plug it back in, wait for the vehicle to thaw, and hopefully get a ride to work. These outlets were installed in front of every building. It was something new that we all had to get used to.

The really big party for the people of Anchorage was the Fur Rendezvous, occurring from the end of February through the beginning of March. It started out with a terrific parade of hundreds of people wearing their fur parkas and fur mukluks (boots). What a marvelous demonstration of furs! We bundled up the kids and went to town for the event. I thoroughly enjoyed watching gigantic men walking in front of their sleds, piled high with furs. Running behind the sled was a tiny, thin Asian man with a long, black braid down his back. The Eskimo blanket tossing was also fun to watch, and something we did not want to try. The blanket was round and made of walrus hide. The Eskimos stand very close to one another, holding the blanket out. One person stands in the middle of it and is tossed as high as possible in order to see the horizon, looking for caribou or any other prey.

Even though we had plenty of warm clothes on, the frigid weather really got to us quickly. I thought I had been accustomed to cold winters back east, but nothing there could prepare me for the sheer, bitter, aching cold in Alaska. Back home we went, glad to be warm again, and hot chocolate hit the spot, especially for the kids.

It was more comfortable watching the activities on TV.

In late summer, we could see the snow creeping down the mountains; by October 11, we had one foot of snow. Since it was dry and cold, it was too light to shovel, and so we had to sweep the snow off the sidewalks. Surprisingly, with all the snow, I missed making snowballs! It was so cold that nothing ever melted; therefore, there was no ice on the roads. It snowed practically every day, making everything clean.

It was Debbie's first day of school on Fort Richardson. School was only two blocks away, but an army school bus was provided—army regulations! Posted on the side window of the bus was a Disney character. The kids were excited, going on the Mickey Mouse bus for instance. That was a very good idea. Someone in the army had a good understanding of children.

They were then driven to the Polaris School, a group of Quonset huts resembling igloos (with low ceilings, warm and cozy). This was perfect for small children. Debbie liked it very much. It was a pleasure to meet Debbie's young first-grade teacher, a very friendly person who recently received her master's degree. We were impressed and thankful. Thoughtfully, she sent work home every night until Debbie caught up to the grade level. This was a pleasant change from the first grade in Anchorage.

All children were taught not to provoke moose by throwing stones or anything else. Keep your distance from them. Do not get between the moose and her young calf; this would be dangerous. If you find yourself in this predicament, go into any house or building, car, or even under a car. Moose have very large bodies but long, thin legs. They can outrun any person or dog. Many dogs met their demise by being trampled by a moose. Having to teach children about the dangers presented by moose seemed like a strange thing, but it was important and very real.

We were not bothered by bears. Thank goodness!

As we moved into winter, we had less daylight. Really, between ten and three o'clock was the only time I could iron. The children went to school in the dark, but the streets were well lit, reflecting off the white snow, which helped. It was dusk when the kids returned home.

The frigid weather was difficult for everyone but mostly for the children. When their mouths were covered, the condensation from their nose and mouth would freeze to the scarf. Chapped lips were a problem. And they had to remember always to wear their winter gear, including hats, boots, scarves, and mittens. I didn't want to take any chance of the kids getting frostbite.

But the winter could also present some wonderful possibilities.

At the end of our street, the mountain range started, making it perfect for skiing. The army recreation department designed a perfect slope for children, making all the skiing equipment available, plus instructors.

The kids could ski after school or early evening. Since it was the winter months and dark, huge floodlights were used, and combined with the white snow, it was as bright as the month of June. The instructors taught the fundamental art of skiing and having fun.

Debbie went skiing every day possible from the age of six to eight years old. She became an excellent skier. Debbie also joined the Girl Scouts. She enjoyed that very much, especially while receiving her badges. Her troop had the opportunity to travel "north to Fairbanks," an overnight trip. She was thrilled to go and had a fine time, except that she didn't care for the extreme cold.

Bill came home from the airfield carrying his winter gear for three weeks of maneuvers. The kids and I watched Bill put on all these clothes. He had several wool shirts and pants (one over the other), big rubber boots that were lined with fur, and a hooded jacket with fur trim around his face. Next were the wool mittens, one pair over the other. The top pair had leather palms with fur on top. This way they could be used to keep his face warm. Finally, the sunglasses, also fur trimmed. At this point, two-and-a-half-year-old Linda started to cry and scream, not recognizing "Daddy." Bill quickly pulled off the glasses and jacket, picked her up, and tried to comfort her. Finally looking at him, she was fine. But I have to admit, he was kind of scary in that getup!

Christmas was coming, so Bill and another pilot friend decided to chop down our own Christmas trees. It was fourteen degrees below zero; he was dressed like an Eskimo with his fur-lined, hooded parka and mittens. After trudging through snow that was waist high, they found the perfect trees. As they were chopping, a moose appeared. The men were rigid, looking up at a huge animal plus its enormous antlers, and afraid to move! After looking them over, the moose slowly walked away. What a relief! But it was very good sense for them to have gone together.

Out in the wild, it is common knowledge to use the buddy system.

Overall, Bill loved his work there. Bill had the ideal job for him. He loved flying, the landscape he saw was magnificent, plus he worked with a group of friendly, happy, and excellent pilots. But it was not all perfect.

CHAPTER 17

⚙

Alaska: Winter Maneuvers

BILL LOVED MOST of his work, but there were the dreaded winter maneuvers, with sub-degree weather and at times dangerous circumstances (living in tents) for three long, cold weeks. The consensus among my friends was that as soon as their husbands left, the kids got sick. For example, the morning Bill was leaving, young Bill fell out of the top bunk bed, hitting his forehead on the edge of a heavy mahogany table. Luckily, the flight surgeon was going with the men, so he looked at young Bill's head. The doctor's diagnosis was a possible concussion. When he walked away he said, "Don't let him sleep." I stood there thinking he would have more to say; he didn't. Bill kissed me good-bye and off they went in order to join the convoy. It turned out, luckily, that young Bill was fine.

In the winter of 1962, someone in the higher echelon put out a mandatory order that all spouses of army personnel stationed at Fort Richardson had to attend a course on survival in Alaska! This was not something I was excited or happy to receive.

The instruction classes were held on Saturday mornings in the post auditorium, and I have to admit that they were very informative. We were taught how to build a lean-to with branches, how to rub sticks together to produce fire, and other survival techniques that would be extremely useful if the wives were caught alone in the wilderness, but they seemed less than needed in Anchorage. The army saw it differently. The classes were all a learning experience, but then we found out that we had to test our talents in the wild!

Here I was in my seventh month of pregnancy, and I was expected to do wilderness-skills training. That was not simply seasickness I experienced aboard ship!

The dreaded day came when we ladies had to bear the sub-zero temperatures and travel by army truck to the snow-covered mountains. I still couldn't believe that I had to do this, given how far along I was in my pregnancy. A good thing did come out of it though—this is where I met Mary (Bernice) Harris.

We all had layers of the warmest clothes on that we owned, including hats, scarves, gloves, and female-type boots, but we were freezing. While the troops were wearing army-issued winter gear, they were still flapping their arms to keep warm. That gives an idea how cold we were.

Our first order: collect branches for a lean-to. But our first job was trying to manage walking in the deep snow with the heavy clothes weighing us down. It was a bit funny for me because I could not bend over! I am sorry to say that I was not much help to my team. It was slowly getting dark and much colder. I wrapped my arms around my stomach, trying to keep the baby warm and to stop shaking. I asked one of the men if there was a possibility to sit in a truck. That idea was denied. I was leaning against a truck's bumper. That did help a little. I felt like a shivering Humpty Dumpty even though I didn't fall.

Finally, the unique exercise came to an end, which I hoped would not be repeated anytime soon! This was not my most enjoyable day as an army wife. I did want to ask someone in the chain of command why he did it in the first place and why he would have a pregnant woman so far along do it as well. I considered it, but I also worried it might cause Bill problems. I still wonder to this day if they do that kind of thing anymore.

Not all such occurrences were so stressful though. One evening Bill and I were dressed for a hobo party at the Officers' Club. Bill put on clothes that didn't match and a faded beach hat. He figured no hobo would have a crew cut, so it was best to wear a hat.

I messed up my hair and added a few pink curlers. Then I put on a bright-red slip, covered by a dark-green button-down-the-front maternity dress. After a few buttons were unbuttoned at my stomach, the red slip was exposed. It looked pretty funny, as if there was a bright-red bowling ball stuck to my body. As we walked into the lobby, there were several bundles of hay along with filthy, smelly chickens running all around. Also, there stood the most offensive, smelly, dirty, ugly *goat* ever! That poor animal never had the pleasure or experience of soap and water. Immediately, we all covered our faces because the stench was too much to endure. The dining room gave out the most pleasurable aroma, but we still could not remove the penetrating smell in our nostrils.

It was an unusual evening since everyone was so out of the usual military appearance. Looking at a high-ranking officer resembling a hobo was comical. We had a good laugh just looking at each other in our silly outfits. After dinner, the master of ceremonies commented on the evening and read the door prize winners. A bottle of wine or champagne and several other prizes were given out. Of course, we all wanted to win the grand prize. The lucky winner was announced, and an ever-so-happy officer ran up to the stage holding up his winning ticket. With that, we saw the backs of two men pulling on a rope that produced the smelly goat! What a shock that was to all of us. We yelled and laughed. A good time was had by all, except the goat winner.

In the spring, outside one of the barracks, stood a clean, well-groomed, handsome, white-haired goat, sporting a banner stating he was the company mascot. How about that!

The troops were always ready for a harmless joke. I know this from my own first-hand experience. I went to the army clinic for my internal checkup. As I was nervously lying flat on my back on the examining table with my feet securely in the stirrups, I looked up at the ceiling. There was a message: "Smile. You could be on *Candid Camera*!"

There were numerous, interesting activities on post to occupy our time: bowling, knitting, and many more, such as curling. It has nothing to do with curling hair. Many of us had never heard of the sport of curling by teams of four. It resembles shuffleboard, but it is played on ice. One team member throws a very large granite stone with a handle down the ice. The other team members, with special brooms, aggressively sweep in front of the stone in order to keep the ice clean. Hopefully the rock would land on or close to the bull's-eye. Several of my friends enjoyed this sport, such as Jan Dukes and Judy Sly.

We both belonged to bowling teams and then bowled together at night with a mixed league. Bill was serious about his game but not me; I was there to talk to my friends and have fun. He wanted me to pay more attention to my game. I tried, but it didn't last long.

After bowling one evening, our team, eight of us, went to our bowling mates' quarters for crab legs. The men went to the docks, and the fishermen gave them plenty of very large legs. We helped put newspapers on the living-room floor, boiled the legs, and then proceeded to stuff ourselves, sitting around the paper. There is nothing like eating fresh, warm Alaskan king crab legs. They are delicious and better than any crab I have had from anywhere else in the states!

No matter where we were in the world, we were never truly far from our family, at least in their thoughts. My mother-in-law, Ella, sarcastically told me she was never the first to hear the news about us because my mother was!

Bill's sister Peggy gave birth in November, her third boy, Jeffrey. We didn't want to take the limelight from her; so we didn't tell anyone, not even my mother, that we were expecting in March. So as not to hurt anyone's feelings, this is what I did. I made a three-by-five-inch card (like a thank-you card) and decorated it in pink and blue balloons and flowers on the front with the word "congratulations." Inside the card it read, "You're going to be grandparents in March! Love Bill and Edythe." The notes went into the mail the same day. Now it was up to the postal service!

March 5, 1962, the *Ed Sullivan* show was on TV as I came downstairs into the living room and announced it was time to go to the hospital. I called Mrs. Maillo, a kind woman who lived next door. As she walked in, we walked out. The kids were happy to finally get a baby sibling.

Luckily, Elmendorf Air Force Hospital was only a five-mile drive away. When we pulled up to the hospital, Bill helped me enter the hospital; the nurses took over, and he went to park the car. When he returned, walking down the hall, the doctor said, "You have a healthy baby boy." Bill replied, "It cannot be. I just got here!" Patrick Michael Gorman arrived, all seven pounds, eight ounces of him, blond hair and blue eyes, in nearly record time. I don't know, but maybe the extreme cold helped! Anyway, mother and child were fine. The children were not allowed to visit me; they had to wait for our homecoming. Debbie and Linda were incredibly happy. Now they had a real-life baby to play with and fuss over. Debbie would even read to infant Patrick while he was in a bassinet.

We didn't phone home very often because of the expense. In order to make a call to the lower forty-eight, we had to ask for a long-distance operator. If we were lucky, Rita Gorman would turn out to be our operator. She married Bob Gorman about a year after our wedding and worked for the phone company. Her voice was like a ray of sunshine, and it was always a treat to hear her cheerful voice. It was a great treat. We were able to get through and tell our family about the wonderful news.

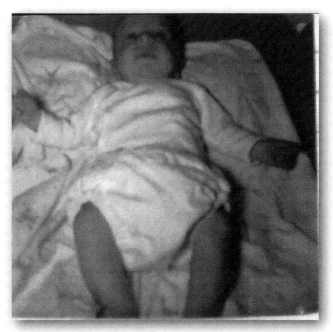

Patrick M. Gorman

Holiday Christmas Card

CHAPTER 18

───── ✧ ─────

Alaska: Fear and Comfort

THE MILITARY STRESSED being prepared in case of any kind of emergency, and this was a time of great tension between the Soviet Union and NATO, led by the United States. Since we were a military family, we felt that tension more than most people. There was always the threat of some kind of attack hanging over everyone's heads. With the fear of any missile crisis, we were instructed to make a space in the basement with assorted items needed in an emergency. Among the supplies we were supposed to amass were canned food, a manual can opener, crackers, cereal, canned milk, candles, matches, flashlights, blankets, and more. We also collected newspapers for human waste, large garbage cans, and big jars of water.

It was also suggested we have things that were meaningful to us, such as a Bible, rosary beads, and special personal mementos. Other essentials that were recommended included toothbrush and paste, comb and mirror, and other sanitary items. For the children, small toys and books were crucial. The only lights that were needed were flashlights and candles.

In October 1962, Bill and I were standing in our kitchen when the house started to shake and canned goods fell off the pantry shelves! We looked at each other in bewilderment. Bill's comment was, "It must be the ice breakup." Then he realized that takes place in the spring.

The Tanana River, just north of Fort Rich, was frozen solid all winter long. The ice breakup was a tremendous event for the Alaskan people. Tickets were sold in order to participate in this natural phenomenon, entering the exact time of the ice cracks right to the precise second. This entire event was supervised by professionals. The excited winner received thousands of dollars! It was party time in Anchorage!

The next day, the *Anchorage Daily Times* ran an article stating there was an eighteen-minute earthquake that jolted the area! No one expressed any alarm, so life continued as normal. It seemed like just another phenomenon that occurred in Alaska that we had to get used to.

At the same time, President Kennedy addressed the nation over the radio. We did not see him until the eleven o'clock news on TV, when he stated the Russians were building offensive weapons in Cuba. We were so pleased how the president sternly handled this war-threatening situation. We were also deeply concerned about how this could turn out. This wasn't simply a possibility of war; but with nuclear weapons involved, this could have meant, if there was a full-scale exchange of nuclear weapons between the two sides, the utter annihilation of life on earth.

The troops were all placed on "high alert," the highest alert possible. We realized the complete seriousness of the situation.

Since Russia is only fifty-five miles from Alaska with the Bering Sea between us, we all definitely felt the tension. This worrisome situation went on for thirteen days. Premier Kruschev of the Soviet Union had apparently believed that he could bully our young president, thinking he was nothing more than a naïve playboy. President Kennedy showed himself to be even stronger than his opponent and a much better man. We now know that many in his Cabinet were urging a direct strike against Cuba and the Soviet Union. This might have ended the world. This young president deserved our thanks and appreciation for thinking of all of us, all the time being a clear and strong leader. We could feel the respect from the soldiers on the base. It was a gigantic relief when the alert was canceled. Amen!

It was a strange time of tension and comfort. While the ground shook in what turned out to be a preamble for the later main event and the fear of war, we not very long afterward made a delightful find. Joan Arend Kickbush was a well-known artist in this area, acknowledged for her oil and watercolor paintings, mostly of Eskimo children. The officers' wives had the pleasure of her attending one of our coffees at the Officers' Club, to which she brought several of her incredible paintings.

We all admired her work, and she had a delightful way about her—the event was most enjoyable. Joan also invited the ladies to her home. We took her up on the invitation and settled on a date. A caravan of us drove north from Fort Rich. In the distance, Mount McKinley started to become visible, just showing the snow-covered peak.

As we arrived at Joan's home, we had the most incredible view of Mount McKinley in its magnificence. It was so regal and one of the most beautiful sights I have ever seen. It is the highest mountain in North America, and its snowy heights seem to rise into the heavens. It was real, but it could have been from a painting from the Romantic period, which tried to capture the sublime. Being near this spectacular mountain made us feel awe.

Approaching the front door, we realized she and her husband, Kick, also an artist, had incorporated a large tree into the front of the house! At first sight, I figured it was a figment of my imagination! It was, however, a demonstration of their artistic imaginations and skills. After entering their awesome home, we saw the other side of the tree, naturally. How artists can bring the distinctive stamp of their creativity into their homes is fascinating.

We were ushered into Joan's studio. What a sight, looking at so many brightly colored paintings of adorable Inuit children. Now for the question—did I want an oil or watercolor painting and what size? I was partial to watercolors. Large paintings were not practical with moving frequently as we did. I finally bought two medium-size eleven-by-sixteen-inch paintings, one of a native mother with a papoose on her back. The other is the father walking along hand in hand with his young daughter as they talk to one another. The main color is blue.

We had an outstanding day.

Bill was pleased with my choice, and they have survived well, given the amount of travelling they have experienced, plus having been in storage several times. I have them hanging in our den now, and they bring back many memories, mostly good ones.

Joan also told us a story about how they built their house, starting with a secure basement where they lived while building the rest of their home. Kick and a few other men went bear hunting while Joan stayed home in the basement, with only the floor/ceiling, which would soon be the first floor of their home, between her and the Alaskan nature's wildness. Joan could hear bears at night walking above her! It was a nail-biting time for her!

"Oh, my" was Kick's reply when he heard Joan's tale regarding the bears because he had returned empty handed.

Eskimo Pictures

CHAPTER 19

------------ ❖ ------------

Alaska: The Coming of Spring

SPRING WAS ARRIVING finally! After a very long winter, we were all looking forward to the coming warmth and especially, the longer daytime. It was so nice to have more time to spend in the sun, especially for the kids. There were flowers blooming and signs of life everywhere. But this also had its interesting qualities.

Springtime also brought a definite aroma all its own. As the snow melted, the moose droppings became evident; henceforth, without the freezing cold to hide their odor, a formidable and awful stench permeated the air. We seemed to be able to smell it wherever we went. Fortunately though, it did not last long and cleared up quickly.

Another advantage of being in Alaska was that we did not have to deal with pests like scorpions. It was a delight to be bug free in the north with the exception of the monstrous mosquitoes. Like so much else in Alaska, even the mosquitoes were larger than those in the lower forty-eight were. But like the moose aroma, these annoying creatures were short lived also.

Now it was our turn to be sponsors for newcomers to Fort Richardson. We met Capt. Ray and Pat Schultz, along with their baby boy, at the airport and drove them around post. We got them all settled in for the night at the guest quarters and invited them for dinner the next evening.

They were a very handsome couple. Pat was a prior beauty queen with wavy black hair and a fair complexion, and she was tall with a shapely figure. She was also a sweet, caring person with a soft-spoken Louisianan accent. We enjoyed being in their company.

Pat and Ray arrived at our quarters as planned. Dinner went well. After clearing off the dishes, I was preparing the dessert. I was shaking a can of whipped cream and accidently sprayed Pat's face, hair, and black dress. Then as I turned, I sprayed the china closet and Ray! This was shocking to all—I was mortified! Meanwhile, our kids were laughing hysterically in disbelief of what their mother did!

As we were trying to clean up, Pat and I exchanged glances, and with that, we busted out laughing. It was an *I Love Lucy* moment, and it cemented our friendship. After a while we thought, "Thank heavens it wasn't Bill's commanding officer's wife."

We had many good times while in Alaska but also some very sad times. One tragedy in particular that I remember occurred when a young married aviator drowned while fishing in a nearby lake. If a person had the misfortune of entering the frigid water, his or her body would start to freeze immediately, disabling the person from moving as hypothermia set in.

Bill's commander appointed Bill and me, plus three other married couples, to pack the widow's belongings after she left for the lower forty-eight. Her friends and neighbors helped pack suitcases and her belongings and safely got her to the airport. The men vacuumed, washed windows, returned slipcovers, and cleaned the bathroom. The women cleaned out the refrigerator and cabinets. Any unopened food would be sent to the orphanage. Other foods were given to neighbors, i.e. opened spices, coffee, tea, and refrigerated items.

Packing their clothes, his uniforms, and her personal female items was depressing. Since we all knew this couple, it was difficult to go through their possessions; we all had the feeling of invading their privacy, but it was something that had to be done.

We had two shipments, first all her clothes, bed linens, kitchen and bathroom items, TV, radio, family pictures, address book, anything we thought she needed immediately. We sent everything to the address given to us. The second shipment was small items like an iron, vacuum cleaner, books, and odds and ends. Of course, their car also had to be shipped.

The quarters were clean and passed inspection. This took about a few days since we all had our own families to care for. Later a memorial service was held for the deceased. It was a very sad time at Fort Rich.

Balancing the sad times were opportunities for experiences that Alaska brought. Bill had a once-in-a-lifetime excursion to fish out in the wild. He and other military men traveled by plane and helicopter to reach the recreation camp for servicemen. It was equipped only with tents for sleeping and a dining hall. All meals were supplied. The men did nothing but fish. Whatever fish they caught would be cleaned, cut to specifications, wrapped, and stored properly until the men were ready to return home.

Bill brought many fish home, but he could not eat this one rainbow trout because its coloring was so bright. So he had it stuffed, and to his delight, he mounted it on the wall for all to admire, mostly himself.

At this point, baby Patrick was about a year old. Everything at first seemed to be normal because I could hear him moving around in his crib after waking up from his nap. As I opened the door, I was startled to see blood on him and his sheet. As I came closer,

I saw blood dripping from his little face from a tiny hole in his cheek. Naturally, my heart leapt when I saw this. I picked him up, held my finger on his little cheek, and ran to the phone to call Bill to come right home. I then called Mrs. Maillo, who came right over to stay with Linda. In a very short time, Bill rushed in, and we went to the Fort Richardson Dispensary.

By this time, both Patrick and I were covered in blood, along with the towels and blanket I had brought along with us.

Thinking Patrick was going to bleed to death, I started to panic.

As we rushed into the dispensary, the nurse, because of all the blood, thought that we had been in a car accident. Suddenly, the doctor appeared and ordered the two nurses, Bill, and me to hold Patrick's arms and legs down on the table. Patrick was happy to lay there until the doctor cauterized the wound with a large needle; then Patrick let his displeasure with the situation be known with an ear-piercing scream that seemed to reverberate throughout the room. Then he calmed down as I picked him up. He was happy and serene, but I wasn't—I was trembling.

Bill and I left and thought that was over, that there would be no more problems.

We were wrong. The next afternoon, Patrick was bloody once more. Back we went to the dispensary, and he had to suffer the cauterizing again. The bleeding started again, evidently, because when he would turn and brush his cheek against the crib sheet, he would knock off the tiny scab. We then went to Elmendorf Air Force Base Hospital where Patrick had been born. This facility was equipped with a much larger staff, equipment, and more specialized doctors. We received an appointment with a pediatrician the next day, and after three procedures over a period of three weeks, that little vein in Patrick's face was fine. The doctor completely closed it.

Only then were Bill and I able to get a good night's sleep again.

It was show time again, but this time it was Bill's turn to perform, plus two other officers, in the Officers' Club as always. The men wore green army fatigues with some alterations!

The outfit started with a huge, dark-green hat made of cardboard for each man to hide his arms and shoulders above them. This made the men bare-chested with their round stomachs exposed down to their hips. The army pants were bloused in big, black army boots. They looked way out of proportion with the big heads and little bodies. Green rolled-up cardboard made the arms with white gloves attached, and ears were taped to the sides. The wives enhanced their husband's nipples with gleaming blue eyes and then heavily applied ruby-red lipstick around the belly button, resembling lips.

As the men marched on stage huffing and puffing, the music was blasting "Bridge on the River Kwai." The men pushed their stomachs in and out so it looked as if they were whistling! At first, the audience could not believe their eyes but then they stood up, yelling, screaming, and waving their arms. What a hilarious show it was!

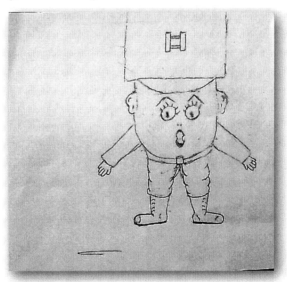

Drawing of "soldier" costume for Officer's Club Play

CHAPTER 20

—✧—

Alaska: Great Sadness

LIFE WAS MOVING along nicely; Bill had just received his clearance to fly floatplanes. This was a major improvement in his work situation, and I was so proud of him. The weather was beautiful and clear. I drove out to Lake Hood with the kids so we could watch him skim over the lake and land in the water right in front of us as he landed the plane perfectly. It was a thrill for all of us.

But then we heard on the radio that President Kennedy had been shot in Dallas, Texas. In the motorcade, Mrs. Kennedy had been riding beside him. After a great deal of commotion and intense speculation that ran throughout the base, the fact was announced—President Kennedy was dead. This was unbelievable. He was the elected leader of our country, a young man whose dynamic personality had inspired many to be the best that they were capable of becoming. He was a brilliant man and a war hero. He had confronted the terrible possibility of nuclear destruction of all people, and he had performed admirably. I am not saying he was perfect, but no one is. He was, however, our president, a man chosen by national election to lead us. For many, he was the symbol of a young and vibrant America that had become the leader of the free world after the horrors of World War II.

A black cloud of gloom came over the post with so many people in shock and disbelief. Even those who did not vote for him were shocked by this horrible act. This sadness was quickly followed by anger! Who would do this to our beloved president?

As always, we had to wait for the 11 p.m. news to bring us the video. Well, this night the stations did not edit the tape; they just ran it, right off the airplane. Our neighbors, the Smiths, came over to watch with us. The pictures were so disturbing and heart breaking; we sat there and openly cried.

During the day, my neighbors would gather and listen to every word that came over the radio. Later we would see on TV what we heard all day. The more we drank coffee and smoked, the more we cried. I will never forget watching the funeral of President Kennedy on TV, especially the image of the riderless horse with the boots in the stirrups backward, symbolizing our fallen leader. It broke my heart to see Mrs. Kennedy in her funeral dress, holding her young children's hands and then to see young John Kennedy salute his father and his sister kiss the coffin. It was heart rending. The country lost a great leader, a wife lost her husband, and two little children lost their father.

I am sure the adults reading this will remember exactly where they were "the day President Kennedy was shot."

CHAPTER 21

Alaska: The Earthquake

THE CONNECTION OF the top-level military authority with everyday life on the base seemed to be more direct than at other places we had lived. When our kids and other neighborhood children were playing in the front yard, one of them would notice Gen. Moore's army car slowly coming down the road. They all recognized the car by the red flags with the two gold stars in the middle attached to the front fenders. Gen. Moore, USA, commanding officer of Alaska, would roll down his back window. The enthusiastic kids proudly stood up and saluted the general. With a big smile, he would return their salute. How awesome that was for the children.

Gen. Moore was very well liked and very friendly. I liked him, and most people did.

The military also performed various services for the civilian population. The pilots would alternate flying via helicopter a priest out to the remote Eskimo villages. They would be overjoyed to have a priest visit so they could have their babies baptized, attend Mass, and be able to confide in a priest. I am sure there were weddings also. Bill enjoyed these trips, and I always wished I could go, but that was not allowed.

The members of the Rod and Gun Club sponsored an Alaskan wildlife buffet in their rustic clubhouse. There was a large assortment; every item was perfectly described. Naturally, there was a large dish of Alaskan king crab and delicious pink salmon, rainbow trout, caribou, and bear. The moose meat, unfortunately, was displayed as <u>moose balls</u>! What a commotion that made! Of course, they were just moose meat ground up and shaped into balls! The chief was having some fun! Very few, however, were eaten.

It was Good Friday at Fort Richardson, Alaska, and I was patiently waiting for Bill to arrive home. I had planned to attend Good Friday service at the Catholic church at three o'clock. Being married to a pilot and trying to live by the clock was impossible. (Cell phones were not available in 1964.)

Bill was late because of the heavy fog. I was disappointed at the time, but as I look back, it was a blessing. Rip Collins was flying with Bill, so he came in and had a drink. We talked for a while; then both men put their glasses on the coffee table, and we all went out to see Rip's new camper. It was a mild day, so we could actually stand around for a few minutes. Rip left, and we came in. I sat on the couch in the living room while Bill was in the recliner. Little Bill was coming up the basement steps when the house started to shake. Bill ran to the kitchen, picked up young Bill, who had been hanging onto the kitchen door, and threw him on the couch. Bill could barely stand up.

There were two young men walking down the street at the time, so I yelled, "Get those men in here." Bill did attempt to stand but the force just threw him, all one hundred and ninety pounds, back down in his chair. Later he said, "It was like standing up in a row boat on a choppy lake."

We were having an earthquake!

The eight family row houses rolled from side to side, also up and down, while making an unbearable, thunderous, crashing roar from all sides and above us! We could do nothing, terrified with uncertainty—were we all going to be killed?

Linda was crying while hanging onto me on one side, Debbie and Bill on the other, and Patrick was sitting on my lap. The couch rolled to the opposite side of the living room, and we watched our TV set roll off the table in slow motion and bounce on the floor. Within seconds, we rolled to the other side, watching lamps and pictures fall and smash. The draperies stood straight out with the windows closed.

Over the roar, I could hear young Bill crying and yelling, "Look, Mom, the cookies are falling." As I looked out into the kitchen, the top cabinet door opened; the Oreo cookies were coming out "fast and furiously" one by one, as a card dealer would deal cards. All of the cabinets opened, and dishes, my good glasses, plus many serving dishes and platters that Bill had sent from Korea smashed to the floor! The refrigerator door opened; it completely emptied. This was one time I was happy we did *not* have fresh eggs in Alaska! Milk, juice, and V8 were running along the floor into the dining room.

By now, we didn't have water or electricity, and night was approaching. I sat watching Rip and Bill's glasses on the coffee table smash into three pieces right in front of me! I could not understand why they didn't slide off the table! We were terrified; it was so devastating and almost unearthly. The ground is not sup-posed to shake. It is supposed to be the foundation upon which we build our lives. Tossing seas and turbulence in the air was normal, but ground shaking and moving was definitely abnormal.

The quake slowly stopped! We just sat there on the couch, still holding onto each other, wondering, and trying to figure out what we had just experienced. I was numb; I didn't even have the good sense to pray! I noticed water dripping from the ceiling. Bill went upstairs to check it out. In the bathroom, he found no water in the toilet because it had all splashed out. Toothbrushes, shav-ing lotion, combs, medicine, and assorted Band-Aids had fallen out of the medicine cabinet into the cracked sink. In the hallway, there was a linen closet that had been half-filled with games; everything had been dumped out in the hall, including marbles, checkers, cards, and more. All the dresser drawers were empty. Dresser tops were swept clean. Clothes and broken glass were scattered, covering the bedroom floor. It felt like a war zone, and we had no idea of the extent of the damage in the rest of the Anchorage area.

We did not know what to expect; it was like being in a spell and afraid to move.

Immediately Bill went down to the basement and brought up the newspapers we had collected for our shelter and placed them on top of all the broken glass and food. He also brought flashlights and garbage cans. From upstairs, he dragged down mattresses, blankets, and pillows and put them on the living-room floor. It was impossible to relax or sleep, not knowing when another quake or the "aftershocks" would start. The kids called them "shakers."

Bill had to report to the airfield. I worried about him since if there was another quake, he would be in danger. Quakes have the power of opening ground and roads wide up, swallowing up anything in their path: buildings, cars, and of course, human beings. It has been known for people to form a human circle/ chain, holding hands so if the ground opened up, the strength of the people kept a person from falling to his or her death.

So there the kids and I were, wrapped up in a blanket in darkness except for candlelight, and I heard a loud knocking at the back door. I could hear the motor of a truck and see flashing lights. I went to the door with a flashlight, and there stood MPs (military police) holding a large container of water. They were checking on all the families for any injuries or problems. They also informed me if another quake hit that we were to stand in a doorway, the strongest structure in a building.

The kids and I had no appetite; our stomachs were upset a little. We were hungry and certainly needed to eat, but the thought of food then turned our stomachs. As we waited for Bill to return home, I continued to pray about his safety.

Bill returned safe and sound; that made me happy and less tense. All aircraft were banned from flying over Anchorage, concerned that the vibrations would cause damaged buildings to collapse.

CHAPTER 22

Alaska: Earthquake Aftermath

THE EXTENT OF the damage from the earthquake was beyond anything I could have imagined. I have never seen war directly, but the destruction from this natural disaster rivaled almost anything that human beings can inflict on each other. Its impact was immense.

JC Penney's department store, only one year old, was destroyed, with cars buried under the building. Some stores had sunk as the street and sidewalks rose. Seward and other towns experienced the tsunami, even as far down as California and Hawaii.

The amount of devastation that Alaska experienced was almost inconceivable. At that time, it was the largest earthquake ever to have hit North America. Albert Rosenfeld, in the April 10, 1964, edition of *Life* magazine, said, "The earthquake that hit Alaska was the strongest ever to hit North America and second most powerful ever recorded [after Chile's 1906 quake]. It unleashed 200,000 megatons of energy, more than 2,000 times the power of the mightiest nuclear bomb ever detonated and 400 times the total of all nuclear bombs ever exploded" (Rosenfeld, 29)[1]. Cities were destroyed, oil tankers were ablaze, and many people were left in a state of shock. It

---

1 Rosenfeld, Albert. "Earthquake in Alaska." *Life*. Vol. 56. No. 15. (April 10, 1964): 26–42.

was as if the entire area was a war zone; the devastation was there, but no enemy soldiers were. Luckily for the people in the city and surrounding areas, the military quickly organized a response-and-rescue team.

The next morning, we all had tetanus shots, and Bill went to the PX and bought a transistor radio. This way we knew what was going on. Twenty-four hours a day, requests asking if anyone knew where their family or friends were came over the radio. "Has anyone seen Mary Smith" or "Joe Black looking for his family." This was so sad. It was almost impossible for me to comprehend the sheer fear and worry that these poor people were experiencing. What we may have lost in terms of material goods was absolutely nothing in comparison to knowing that my family was safe. I felt so bad for those people who had lost friends and family to death or had people missing. What a terrible situation that was.

Since it was Good Friday, the schools were closed. People had been out shopping, not at work, or attending church services. The Anchorage High School collapsed during the earthquake. Thank God that the school was not in session. As bad as this quake was, it would have been so much worse if it had struck on an ordinary day when most people would have been at work or school.

Later I found out that many statues fell and smashed at the church; I am glad I was not there. The people in church must have thought the world was ending.

Also, Mary Harris had a premature baby girl before the earthquake. When the quake happened, part of the hospital sank; therefore, the babies were moved to a safer part of the hospital. It was a nerve-wracking time for her family and her. Fortunately, the baby grew and became a very healthy, adorable little girl.

During the quake, troops were running out of barracks in their underwear. Women (some half-dressed, carrying babies) were screaming while coming out of houses.

Before the quake, I ran into Doris and Bud Wheeler. What a surprise that was! We were classmates in Millburn High. Also, they had been class sweethearts. Neither one of us knew the other one was in the service, let alone in Alaska. After the quake, it was impossible to make a call to the states. Doris called the Red Cross and explained about her mother's illness; she got a call through to Millburn, New Jersey. After talking with Doris, her mother, Mrs. Fandetta, called my parents. What a relief for my family to know we were fine. I will be forever indebted to you; thank you, Doris.

I am convinced that everything happens for a purpose!

One thing that kept me on edge was that even though the main quake was over, aftershocks, sometimes called shakers, would continue. As I was feeding Patrick in his highchair one noontime, a very strong tremor started. In my panic, I could not get Patrick out of his chair, so I dragged the chair, with him in it, to the door! It didn't last long, but they always shook me up, and it took a while for me to calm down. When I put Linda down for a nap, she wanted to keep her shoes on so her feet would not be in the snow! (That's a three-year-old.)

Debbie would say after school, "Gee, Mom, did you feel that shaker today?" Most of the time I didn't, and the school was just a few blocks away. Often during the night, Bill and I woke up to a soft rattling sound from the dresser's drawer pulls. As the noise worsened, the house would shake. Bill would grab Pat out of the crib as I managed the other kids, and we would feverishly run downstairs to the front door, bunched together, shivering from fright! The uncertainty persisted. Was this another strong earthquake or merely a tremor? Fortunately, they all settled down slowly and stopped. There we stood, wide awake with our hearts running rapidly, but we were relieved. Now we had to try to relax and hopefully sleep. The kids were more than happy to climb back in their safe, warm beds. They seemed to adjust to the tremors much faster than we adults did. I think it is a testimony to the innate strength and ability of children to adjust to new situations.

Life was slowly settling down for us, but not for the town of Anchorage. There was a great deal of work to be done. The repair and rebuilding immediately got underway.

There were times I was sure the house was moving. Bill and the other pilots in the office had the same problem. They hung a string of paperclips from the overhead light. We did the same thing at home. If the clips did not move, you knew it was your mind playing tricks on you.

Whenever a serious weather event occurs, it comes and goes. Not an earthquake—it hangs around, tainting your nervous system with tremors! Some of the army wives had to return to the lower forty-eight with their children. I am sure they didn't want to leave their husbands. Unfortunately, that is how nerves can affect someone.

Bill was awaiting orders since we should have been leaving Alaska in June. I was praying we would go to any place *but Fort Benning, Georgia.* Many of our pilot friends got orders for Fort Benning; we figured the infantry was building up the troops for a large movement. Possibility—Vietnam?

Bill's orders arrived for Fort Hood, Texas. Those orders were fine with us.

It was time to say farewell to fascinating Alaska with the dazzling Northern Lights, snow-like crystallized sugar, and thirty-five-pound cabbages. This time we hired a professional cleaning company; they were approved by housing, so this way we didn't have the concern of checking out.

Our friends dined and wined us the last weeks and held the usual farewell party at the O'Club. Some of them wished they were returning to the lower forty-eight with us. We settled into the guest quarters. It had a big kitchen for all the transit personnel. We would have breakfast and lunch there, with dinner at friends' homes. It also had a washer and dryer available. That was a blessing.

It was a bright, sunny June night when we boarded a huge plane. Destination: Seattle, Washington! Patrick was two years old, so Bill had matchbox cars in his pocket in case Patrick was restless. He never needed them since he slept in my arms for the complete time.

As we flew over the glistening snow-topped mountains with pink-and-blue sky behind them, over and over I kept telling the kids to take a good look because "you'll never see this spectacular view again!"

We were in Seattle, travelling with about four suitcases; we put them in a locker in order to eat. When we returned, Bill found that one suitcase was not ours. It belonged to a soldier from Fort Rich. After answering the page, he returned to the lockers, finding he had our suitcase full of girls' clothes. We had army uniforms. We thought it was a funny thing that happened.

We went on our merry way and arrived in Newark, New Jersey, with our families meeting us.

CHAPTER 23

Fort Hood, Texas (1964)

As we drove to Fort Hood, Texas, from New Jersey, I was reflecting on our outstanding visit we had had with family and friends. I was surprised by how much my nieces and nephews had grown. Then there was Peggy's first born, a handsome, red-haired boy named Jerry. Everyone had been so happy to see us, and we had been delighted to see our families. It seemed as if the family was ever expanding and always moving as well; it was wonderful to be able to gather together, something that we could never be sure would happen.

Being home was a warm and lovely feeling. Unfortunately, we were very conscious of any loud noise or movement, such as a heavy truck going down the street. The kids would immediately look at each other, Bill, or me. "Quake?" we would all think. It took a long time to get over that fear.

We were invited to travel into New York for the World's Fair. There was no way we would think of going. Our nervous systems could not endure the extreme noise and confusing climate. That earthquake left a deep emotional scar in all of us.

Since we didn't have fresh milk or eggs in Alaska, we could not get enough of them. Bill was thrilled to have milk for his Dunk 'Em Oreos. Egg-salad sandwiches were my hang up. We also bought a new Buick station wagon with air conditioning, so we had a comfortable drive south. Fortunately, we rented a small, air-conditioned ranch house on Chaney Drive, Killeen, Texas, on a dead-end street. The best part was that the Catholic church and school were right behind us. It was a perfect situation!

Our first concern was scorpions; while they were not as large as the beasts in Yuma, they were still very present. Our house was set on a slab of concrete, and the scorpions liked cool concrete, making them an ever-present threat! The kids said their night prayers while kneeling on their beds. Along with their slippers, we didn't have to worry about them getting stung.

Our next-door neighbors were Dr. Joe Adducci, an obstetrician, and his wife, Mary Anne, who happened to be a nurse. They were both very friendly and caring people and about our age. We enjoyed their company, and our children got along with their two boys, Chris and Gregory.

Debbie and young Bill started school, but Linda was not yet six years old, so she stayed home with Patrick. That was fine; she had two-and-a-half-year-old Patrick to play with, her own baby!

Similar to our experience in Alaska, in this new place we had things to get used to. I never saw mud like Texas mud. It would stick to the kids' shoes like brown glue, inches thick. It became like thick glue that grew and grew, like something out of a bad monster movie. Eventually, I figured out the best way to handle this mud situation. After the mud dried, we hammered it off! The kids thought this was great fun, especially using a hammer. Another thing they enjoyed was playing with Texas horny toads! They were kind of scary little critters, but the children were not afraid of them.

In September, Bill and I found out he would be leaving in October for the "major air-assault testing maneuvers" announced by the Pentagon. These training and testing events would be held in North and South Carolina and Georgia. This was a large operation with pilots attending from all over the country. Bill would be gone from October 14 to November 12.

To say I was upset with this news would be an understatement. I wasn't simply troubled by this plan; I was furious! I wasn't mad at Bill; I was angry with the army! We had been stationed here for only about six weeks! I thought that we might have been able to look forward to a little stability, both for the kids and for myself. Oh well, that's one of the downfalls of army life. We had to always expect the unexpected.

I guess I was still holding some nervousness from the earthquake. I could not sleep when Bill was on duty out on post, listening to the howling coyotes in the distance, plus the sound of tumbleweed rolling around in the wind. I felt so safe at Fort Rich, but not here. Thinking it would make me feel safer at night, Bill proceeded to nail the windows shut. I could get out, but no one could enter.

Before Bill left, he came home with a whistle in his hand. It seems when the men are on maneuvers, the troops left behind enjoy themselves by telephoning the wives with heavy breathing and obscene language. It seemed to be a very strange form of entertainment. We were issued whistles; if we received a call like that, we were to blow the whistle as hard as possible. The shrill noise would damage their eardrum, making them report to sickbay. It worked very well; one soldier was caught that I know of, but it was highly likely that there were more.

Regarding the telephones, there was no such thing as a private line. There were "party lines" with at least three other families on the same line. If I wanted to make a call, I'd pick up the receiver, and usually someone was talking. So I would have to hang up and try sometime later. I could not leave the receiver off the hook, so I buried it in a box full of material during the night. While Bill was gone, I tried to keep composed. In the evening, I did a paint-by-numbers picture; concentrating on creating that image helped.

Fort Hood had two armored divisions. It was the largest post in the United States, meaning it had thousands of troops. Bill's company commander's wife asked me to fill in for her several times, since there were many coffees, teas, and luncheons to attend. This gave me the chance to meet many more wives. I was invited by a colonel's wife to attend the "Change of Command" ceremony for the general leaving Fort Hood. I was a mere major's wife. She was a friendly lady, so we got along just fine. The dress code was dress, hat, stockings, high heels, and white gloves. We sat in bleachers under the blazing Texas sun watching thousands of troops march in formation in front of us, plus hundreds of tanks, trucks, heavy artillery on the ground, and aircraft overhead. The noise was deafening, and the dirt and dust flying on us was just too much! After that, we were obliged to make our way down to the tent where the general and his wife stood so we could wish them well. Our reward for this event was a cookie and a small cup of punch. We were so thirsty and covered in dust that we couldn't get out of there fast enough. Never again! Later, we laughed about that day!

It was a sunny day, but slowly the sky darkened, and the wind started to blow. I was told by a neighbor that in case of a tornado, open windows to allow the wind to blow through the house. It seemed like a good idea and a reasonable safety precaution. Well, I opened the kitchen window, and I got a face full of sand and pebbles. It even blew the small items off the counter, so I quickly closed the window. This situation was getting serious; I had the kids get under my double-size bed and instructed them to hold onto the legs of the bed. Holding Patrick, I followed them underneath. It became darker and noisier from the wind. The kids were a bit frightened, and I was very worried, but I didn't let on because I didn't want the children to become even more scared. After a few minutes, it was all calm. When I was certain that everything was all right, I let them come out from under the bed. The kids didn't think too much of it, and they thought of it as some kind of game or adventure, but they had no idea how bad it could have been.

In addition to the worry about tornadoes, it was so hot and humid. It seemed that wherever we went, Bill and I found extreme weather conditions to deal with. Mary Anne and I would sit outside and watch the kids play or put them in the kiddy pool. When young Bill and Debbie came home, I always felt better when they were with me. I just could not get the idea of a sudden tornado out of my mind, and I wanted to be sure that the kids were safe.

That night young Bill started in with a temperature, so Joe, Dr. Adducci, examined him and found that Bill had pneumonia. Instead of admitting Bill to the hospital on post, Joe treated our boy at home. Joe came over to check on Bill at 7:00 a.m. before he went to work, at lunchtime, after work, and at night. Mary Anne, an RN, was in and out all day checking on Bill. They gave him such outstanding and nurturing care, even more than he would have received in the hospital. I do not know what I would have done without them. Bill and I will always be in their debt.

Bill and I wrote letters to each other every day, plus he was allowed a phone call when young Bill was sick. Thank goodness, young Bill was back to himself in no time.

Joe treated all of us to the small traveling circus in town. Mary Anne and I got to laughing. She was expecting a baby (Steven) at the time, so here was Joe walking along with a pregnant wife, six kids, and me. How funny did that look! The kids loved having a fun night. They really needed it after all the stress they had been through.

While Bill was away, Debbie made the sacrament of confirmation, and young Bill made his first Communion. These are two important sacraments; we had a little party, but not having their father there left a big void.

Thank God, Bill returned home before Thanksgiving. We were worried he would not make it, but all turned out well. On Christmas Eve, Joe had Santa Claus stop at our house. Chris and Gregory were there also. Fun and excitement was had for all the kids, including the older adult kids.

It was a tradition that the commander, most likely a general depending on the size of the post, had a New Year's Day reception. This event was mandatory attendance. This was a large inconvenience for many of us since we had been at the Officers' Club the night before. Bill's company was scheduled to appear as a group at 10:30 a.m. in full dress uniform with the ladies wearing party dresses, hats, stockings, high heels, and naturally, white gloves.

New Year's Day is a day of obligation for Catholics, so there was no question that we were going to attend Mass. We had to wake the kids up early, have breakfast, dress them in their church clothes, and go to early Mass. When we returned home, we quickly changed them into play clothes and ran them across the street to the babysitter, Mrs. Lopez. This lovely lady was a lifesaver for us. Then Bill changed into his uniform, and I dressed as well. We drove out to the Officers' Club and stood in line to shake hands with the general and his wife, have a cup of punch, and try to look awake. By the time we got home, had the kids run across the street, and changed to comfortable clothes, we were exhausted! And it was only noontime. I really felt sorry for the general and his wife; they had to stand there all day and shake hands.

A short while after New Year's, the Officers' Club was having a "Western Get-together Night." A week before the party, I became a blonde! I was tired of mouse-brown hair, so naturally I had to shampoo my hair. Well, when I did, it turned bright red! Surprise, surprise! Bill just looked at me and smiled. (He never knew what to expect from me.) I ended up going as Miss Kitty from *Gunsmoke*, an old western TV show.

PS, I was blond again the next week, but being a redhead was kind of fun.

It seemed to be that one event followed quickly on the next. A spectacular dinner dance, with cocktails at the Officers' Club, was given by Bill's commanding officer. It was strictly a formal evening. The men were dressed in full, decorated dress uniforms, showing off all their colorful medals. The ladies wore full-length evening dresses, a magnificent sight.

We were all informed not to consume much liquid since no one could excuse himself/herself during dinner. Each couple had their own white-gloved server standing behind them to tend to their needs. It was a full-course meal from soup to nuts, including the perfect wines accompanying each course. After that elegant dinner, we were served liquors of our choice.

Like the old tradition, the men were ushered into the smoking room and served brandy and cigars. We ladies were escorted into a room reminiscent of a living room and treated to petit fours and demitasse. It was very impressive, and it was the most elegant affair we ever attended. This will always be an awesome memory for me! We all danced the night away! In the grand tradition of elegant balls, the dancing was formal, ranging from waltzes to fox trots. There were elegant men and ladies whirling around like something out of the Victorian age.

Our living situation was never quite what we wanted. We had been here for about a year, and finally we were number one on the post's housing list. We were excited about moving on post; Mary Anne and Joe were already on post. Well, that never happened! Ironically, just when it seemed likely that we would be able to move, changes were dictated.

Bill received orders for Fort Benning, Georgia! This was just what we had been dreading. Bill called Rip since he was stationed at Fort Benning. Kiddingly, I told him we wanted to rent a large five-bedroom, two-and-a-half-bath house with a large living room and a big den! Oh, yes, also a maid and gardener. I was laughing all the time I was talking to him! It seemed to be the best approach to try to stay as light hearted as possible.

Rip returned our call the next night. He had everything I ordered down the street from him and Jerry. We could not believe it; we rented it sight unseen. Mary Anne and Joe invited us over for dinner after the packers left. That was very thoughtful of them. The week before, the officers' wives presented me with a sterling-silver bookmark. The colonel's wife that I represented at coffees and luncheons gave me a small silver tray perfect for calling cards, which was engraved with "Thanks, Edi." I really appreciated that gift and told her so; it was really my pleasure.

Thankfully, the packers came again to ship everything to Fort Benning.

Off we went to Fort Benning, Georgia, knowing Vietnam was in our future. We didn't want to talk about it, but it hung over our heads like an unacknowledged headache.

Fort Hood, Texas

CHAPTER 24

Fort Benning, Georgia

WE HAD AN uneventful trip except for the pouring rain, high winds, and dark sky, which was perfect tornado weather! Having experienced this possibility before, we understood the potential danger this represented. Bill and I were very concerned. At one point, we pulled off the road, along with all the cars in front and behind us. Several cars drove down a farmer's lane and parked beside the barns. It was a very frightening time because we realized that simply parking did not provide much protection if a tornado did hit. But at that point, there was little more that we could do except pray. After a while, the storm slowly moved away from us. The intense black clouds moved into the distance, and to our delight, the sun came out. Thank God!

When we arrived, the settling in to our new home was simpler than we had experienced in the past. Thanks to Rip and him finding a place for us, we were able to move in quickly and efficiently. We were very happy when looking at our new house. We had assumed a very modest living situation since that was what we were accustomed to. When we saw the house, we realized that it was much bigger than we had imagined. The den was a very large room, which made Bill very happy. The next day, we drove into town and purchased den furnishings. The rest of the home was spacious, with enough bedrooms, a nice kitchen, a large dining room, and a beautiful living room. A day later, our household shipment arrived, and the house looked more like home.

Bill reported to work at the airfield the next day. He returned with the news the post was on alert, preparing to invade Vietnam. We both thought this was likely to happen, but we had not actually said it. It seemed as if not talking about it might keep it from happening, but of course, that was wrong. Once we heard that the post was on alert and why, everything became entirely different. Now the possibility of war had become the likelihood of actual fighting.

I kept thinking, "My husband is actually going to be in combat— possibly not to return alive!" The tears rolled down my face, just like right now as I write this. I tried not to cry, but I could not control my feelings. Bill and I were in love, had been through so much together, and had faced everything as a couple, and now there was a chance we would not only be separated but also ripped apart if he died. I just couldn't stand the idea that he might be killed. He was the love of my life, and he held my heart; he was the center of my world. I couldn't stand the thought of losing him. Bill held me, trying to comfort me and saying, "I love you with all my heart, and I'm sorry we have to face this, but we'll be OK. We'll be OK, Doll," as he hugged me tight and patted my back. Unfortunately, we both knew that going to war was a risk everyone who joins the military faces, but I think we, or at least I, didn't think it would happen to us. We didn't tell the kids right away since this was "top secret."

Very soon after we found out about the alert, my mother called asking if she and Dad could come down. Since it was summer, the kids were out of school. I really didn't know what to say, most of all over the phone. I could not bring myself to lie to her by making up some story why they could not come. So a visit was arranged. I did wonder how this would go since the worry and tension both in our home and on the base was palpable.

They arrived by train from New Jersey. My mother made the best gingerbread with thick, chocolate, homemade icing, and she disembarked the train carrying gingerbread. We were all surprised since everyone in the family loved it, and it was my favorite bread (more like a cake). I still cannot make one like hers. Somehow, carrying this present of gingerbread was almost like a magic talisman that helped to repel the tension for a bit. I was happy they were with us; they helped to ease the strain.

I was then faced with a huge dilemma: I had to decide if I wanted to stay in this big split-level house while Bill was away for a year or move back to Wharton, New Jersey. I really didn't want to be there alone, watching the green staff car moving slowly down the street and checking out house numbers. It would be very eerie, worrying if the car would stop at my house with the message starting with "The United States of America is sorry to inform you," etcetera or wording close to that. As bad as the situation might be, that staff car would seem to be the specter of death hovering over everyone. This possibility was the toughest part of being a military wife: facing the uncertainty of my husband's safe return from combat.

I chose to return to Wharton. I could live with Ella and Hen until I found a place of my own. I would rather be home if bad news would come. By now, it was only a month before Bill would leave with the US First Cavalry Air Mobile Division. A good thing was that Bill would be flying the Huey helicopter, not on ground duty with the infantry. I hoped that assignment would give him a layer of safety that he would not have had if he had been in the infantry.

We once again had the moving van come in to start packing. The same day, Bill came home with approximately three thousand dollars, representing advance pay and travel pay. As the furniture was crated for storage, Bill and I stood in the kitchen wondering where we could hide this money until the packers left. We put it in the tea canister that fit in the bigger canister: flour, sugar, coffee, and small tea canisters—this was perfect. We all busied ourselves cleaning and packing. The men left for the day to return the next day to finish up. We proceeded to change clothes in order to have dinner and check into the motel. First, we planned to count the money and plan as to how much money Bill would need and how we would use it in the future. I went in the kitchen and the canisters were packed, boxed, and taped. There were about eight large boxes marked "kitchen." We just laughed, knowing the money was safe!

It was a good idea that we had because the packers were very fast, and they did the kitchen that very day!

The next morning, the packers returned with a slim-built black man who was in charge. I explained about the money, and in a flash, he knew the exact box, quickly tore the box open, and appeared with the canister set. He handed them to me from his shaking hands. As I opened the canister and pulled out the money, he was overcome with joy, saying, "Thank the Lord." We all were so happy for him, and every time he would pass me during the day, he would say, "Thank the Lord." He was such a good man.

Finally, all the boxes to be stored in Dover, New Jersey, near the Gormans' home, were packed on the moving van.

Once we knew Bill would be leaving, I bought new underwear for him since it all had to be dyed "OD—olive drab" color along with handkerchiefs, socks, and other white items. This, of course, was so the enemy could not detect them. It went against my grain to submerge pure-white new and old items into olive-drab dye! But I did it! And they all came out very, very drab.

We also packed Bill's uniforms, boots, flight helmet, flight jacket, and other items into a large duffle bag. This would be left at Rip's until Bill returned to Fort Benning, where he would depart for Vietnam. I also had to pack summer and winter clothes in the car for the kids and myself since I didn't know how long we would be with Ella and Hen. This was a time of great uncertainty in our lives. Everything seemed to be in constant motion and ongoing flux.

My parents drove back to New Jersey with us instead of returning by train. When we departed from Fort Benning, the car was packed to the brim and suitcases were tied to the roof, plus four adults and four children were crammed into the inside of the station wagon. What a sight we must have been, like something out of *The Grapes of Wrath*! Only I am glad to say that we were not impoverished like those poor people from Oklahoma on the road during the dust bowls in the Great Depression.

That night we traveled to Atlanta and stopped at a motel close to the airport. We were so exhausted, but we could not sleep since the planes went right over our room. Knowing that Bill was leaving soon for Vietnam, that we still had to make it home to New Jersey, and that we had to be parted for a year, the uncertainty of our lives was overwhelming. My mind went crazy over all the horrible things that could happen. *Would Bill come back alive? Would he come back healthy? What would I do if he were killed? How would I face life without the love of my life? What would our kids do without their father? How will I stand it, not knowing if Bill is safe or not?* As much as I tried to put on a brave face for the sake of Bill and the kids, I knew deep in my heart how worried I was and would continue to be. All I could do was sob and hold onto Bill tighter and tighter. Bill kept holding me and said, "It's going to be OK, Baby Doll. Take one day at a time." There was nothing else to do, and nothing I could do to change the situation. I would worry about Bill until the day I saw him come home safe from Vietnam.

The kids were fine, as always, traveling, but my father was a royal pain in the neck! He was either was thirsty, was hungry, or needed a bathroom stop. The trip was long, but we made it, happy to get Dad home.

Bill only had a week or so before he had to leave. We were staying with Ella and Hen then, and that week went by entirely too fast. I was hoping that each day could be made to seem like a month, but the opposite happened. It seemed that no sooner had the day begun then we were getting ready for bed.

The day came when Bill had to leave. Many of the relatives came over to express their best wishes. They all sat in the back-yard as if they were all in mourning after a funeral. I could not stand it! Rather than seeming like support, they were acting as if his fate had already been decided. In an odd way, this negative attitude gave me strength because I disagreed with them. The kids and I kissed Bill good-bye. Bill and I did not want to let go of each other.

Jerry, Peggy's husband, drove Bill to the Newark airport. I could not bear to hear one more person say to me, "Poor Edythe," as they hugged me. I could have screamed! I felt like shouting, "We will be fine!"

So I said to the kids, "Let's go over to church, light a candle, and say a prayer for Daddy." That helped to be alone with the kids because we were a team!

CHAPTER 25

―― ⁌ ――

Wharton, New Jersey, and Vietnam

LIVING WITH ELLA and Hen was very stressful, mostly at dinnertime. While I was extremely grateful to them for inviting us to stay in their home, it was also difficult to not be in charge of our place of living. I had been part of a couple taking care of our home for so long that it was difficult to live under someone else's roof. It certainly didn't help that young Bill had a way of pushing Ella's buttons. It kept me on pins and needles. I was, however, not the only one feeling the stress. It was very trying for Ella, with four kids and me living with them suddenly. They had gone from a quiet household of two older people to a noisy home of seven people. What a change that was for them.

Every day I would check the paper for apartment rentals. I kept coming up empty until one day I answered an advertisement and went over to check it out. It was perfect. Sally and Irving Friedman were the owners of this large, splendid home. They were both very friendly people. Irving was a tall, black-haired, handsomely dressed man, and Sally was fashion minded, swam at the Y every day, and was artistic. I was relaxed with them immediately, and that helped enormously.

Irving showed me through the house, which was divided into two apartments; my side was the bigger one. The kitchen was remodeled, and it was a big enough for a washer/dryer. There was a small powder room, and a sizeable dining room, which I turned into a den. The living room was bright with French doors opening to the semicircle white porch. I loved it! Both rooms had fireplaces that were closed up. It was a beautiful place.

Upstairs were two big bedrooms and a large master bedroom. The sunken bathroom was unique, having two steps down, with the old claw-foot tub and cottage-like windows along one side. I would be able to take a bath with the small windows open. It also had a corner walk-in shower.

The third floor was a spacious lounge with colorful, cushioned bamboo furniture and a standard pool table. This wonderful addition to the living space was something I would never have searched for, but it came in very handy. Later, Irving taught young Bill and Debbie how to play pool.

At this point, I was dumbfounded! What a magnificent house. I just had to move in as soon as possible. I thought I had seen it all until I had the pleasure of touring Sally and Irving's side of the house. Their kitchen was small with a huge fireplace, called the summer kitchen years ago. I got a warm, homey feeling from the entire place.

I am sure my mouth dropped open as I entered their living room (originally the music room). It was breathtaking! The walls displayed oil paintings of all sizes placed perfectly. Every piece of antique furniture was well polished and made of mahogany or cherry with perfect upholstery. The best thing was the grand piano! I thought we could never afford such a grand rental, but I rented it immediately since it was only $175.00 a month! I made sure they realized I had four children! That was fine with them, thank goodness.

I was so excited—thrilled was more like it, but I had to get myself together before I told Ella and Hen. Of course, Ella didn't like the news. I really didn't know why, but I did not care. I would have thought that she would be happy to have her home back, but she could be contrary sometimes. The kids, however, were so excited! The next day I called in the moving company, and in a few days, we were moved in. After checking all the boxes, it all went well.

Before I left Ella and Hen, I changed all the beds and cleaned the bedrooms and the bathroom; I didn't want her to say I had left a mess. The kids and I had a wonderful time opening the boxes, finding the bed linens, and making beds. By the time we finally sat down around the kitchen table to eat, we said our before-meals prayer and thanked God for everything. I was more than happy to sit there looking at my kids and knowing we would be safe here. Bill was relieved and happy to hear how well things were going.

CHAPTER 26

Vietnam (1965)

BILL WROTE HE was presently at the "tea" plantation (years ago, a French tea plantation) west of Plei Me, and that he would be leaving the next day for An Khe. Bill was with the 227th Aviation Battalion (1st Cavalry Air). He never wrote me what he was actually doing, but I knew flying helicopters over there was dangerous. I know that Bill didn't want me to know the reality of what was going on in Vietnam, but I felt compelled to learn as much as I could. The 227th Aviation Battalion was used to move soldiers directly into and out of immediate combat zones at the height of treetops, some of them having the fiercest fighting in the war. And Bill was right in this unit flying one of those helicopters. I felt a lot like the wives of the soldiers in World War II, having to stay home but wanting to feel as if they were somehow still with their husbands. We had been in love since we knew each other, and that connection was just as strong even though we were separated by half a world.

I watched the news in the evening, seeing all the helicopters in combat. Walter Cronkite was the main television news announcer at the time, the man trusted by most Americans, and I hoped he would give the real news, even though sometimes I was very afraid of what I might see or hear. I knew I shouldn't watch, but I was drawn to it. I guess I was foolish enough to think I would see Bill, but I never did.

Before Bill left for Vietnam, we decided to purchase new living room end tables and a coffee table. The morning these items were to arrive, Linda complained of a stomachache. I thought she wanted to be the first to see the furniture. At my request, even though she was still in pain, she spent the day in bed until Debbie and young Bill came home from school at 3:30 p.m.

We went to the doctor to find that Linda had appendicitis! I felt so bad and still do. She was admitted to Dover General Hospital, and after several blood tests, Linda had her appendix removed at 8:30 p.m. She was a true champ; she never fussed or cried. I explained what Doc. Bertha would do. She would sleep, and it was not going to hurt. I'd be right there when she woke up! I was so proud of her, of how brave my little girl was in what could easily have been a terrifying time for her.

When Bill received my letter a week later, he was able to get an emergency call through because he felt bad about not being here. He was already in the midst of making connections out of Vietnam and heading into Cambodia to come home. However, Linda would probably be back to school by the time he arrived home.

The next couple of days, the kids would go to Ella and Hen's after school. Linda never complained; she enjoyed her roommate and the little boy that swallowed a penny. She would be home before Christmas.

Christmas was coming, and how I would manage this holiday without Bill was on my mind. Bill always said, "Doll, handle one day at a time." As I looked for the Christmas decorations, I found that I didn't have any! Evidently, the box was lost in one of the shipments. But my Aunt Florence rescued us by giving me all of hers since she moved into a smaller apartment. I was upset; we lost all our stuff, most of all the things we had for our first Christmas together—especially the "Honeymoon Express," a wind-up tin train that ran on a track. We bought it in the 5&10 cent store while at flight school.

Felice and Vince arrived, to my surprise, with a Christmas tree and stand, which was such a thoughtful thing to do. I was happy since I didn't know how I'd accomplish the task. We put the lights on, and Vince put on the little Christmas balls and the angel on top. They went home, and the kids came home from school to see a Christmas tree in the house! They were delightfully surprised! They all helped, even little Patrick, placing the rest of the balls, but when it came time for the tinsel, they thought it looked OK in bunches. I thought it best for me to handle that job myself.

My mom and dad were there. Dad went to bed, so we worked with the tinsel. I could not figure out how I could reach the top of the tree with the tinsel. I took the broom on the bristly end, laying strands of tinsel on it, walked up on the three-step footstool with broom in hand, and laid the tinsel on the branches. It worked! All the time, my mother was chuckling. She remarked how Bill would have loved to see that act.

I don't think many people realize how military wives improvise all the time.

While Bill wasn't there in person to be a part of the Christmas festivities, I was sure to remember every detail so that I could tell him about it in a letter. Besides, I always felt that he was with me all the time.

The Friedmans, being Jewish, experienced their first Christmas tree, decorations, and most of all a wreath on the door. They were such wonderful and open people. Not only did they help to bring joy into our family, but also I think we brought some happiness into theirs as well. It felt as if we were all part of a family. It was fun and heartwarming watching the activities and the children playing.

On Christmas Day, Mom and Dad came over. I also had Ella and Hen over, so with the nine of us, the day was festive. It was a busy and happy time with the opening of gifts, having dinner, and watching the kids play with their toys. I really had dreaded this day a lot without Bill being there, but it all turned out well. I wish we had computers in those days. Bill and I were happy he could make one phone call per year! So we depended on the old-fashioned means of letter writing.

A few days after Christmas, Jean called, crying, and said, "Toady was killed in action." I was speechless; I didn't know what to say! There was silence, and then we cried for a long time—it seemed like that anyway. They didn't have any children. What a terrible time that was. We all dreaded this and hoped we would never hear it.

I wanted to go down to Fort Benning to be with her, but I could not bring myself to leave the kids. I never wanted to be away if we would receive bad news. All I could think was "Was Bill with him?" The kids were in school, except Patrick, and that was a good thing. Now I had to collect myself in order to give Ella and Hen the bad news. When I went into their house, they were sitting in the living room watching a soap opera.

As I told them about Toady, Ella stood up, waving her arms above her head while pacing and yelling at me, "We're next! We're next!"

And I screamed back to her, "No, we are *not*!" This did not go well at all.

Hen sat there ever so quietly sobbing, and Ella and I stopped yelling at each other, even though we were really yelling at the fate that took Toady and not each other. Ella and I slowly collapsed into chairs, and then the three of us just sat there and cried. They loved Toady, with his charming southern accent and his loving nature. For the next couple of days, I prayed with all my heart for two things: for Toady and his soul and that my doorbell would *not* ring!

This was an extremely difficult time for us, and we slowly dealt with it by trying to do the ordinary things in life: watching over kids, helping with homework, cooking, and making meals. These very prosaic activities helped me get through the pain of losing a close friend, coupled with the fear that Bill might be next.

Springtime finally came, and Linda made her first Communion. My mother made a beautiful white, embroidered dress for her. Linda was thrilled because she had a "swinging around dress." I wish Bill could have seen her. He would have been so proud of her and so happy to see his little girl celebrating this very important religious milestone. I know he was proud of her where he was.

Bill wrote he would go to Cambodia in the summer on an R&R, a week of rest and relaxation. This was the way the service gave the troops a mini-vacation. He said he would try his best to call and give me the dates when he knew he would be calling from Cambodia. He wanted to keep me informed of what he was doing as much as he possibly could, even though I understood that would be very difficult, at best.

The school year for the kids had gone well, and I had helped a couple days a week at school wherever I was needed. It was fun. I knew what was going on, and I was around the kids. It was good to be occupied this way.

I also joined the Wives' Club at Picatinny Arsenal even thought there was a problem at first. A few of us had husbands in Vietnam, but the Officers' Club would not yet let us join. This definitely did not seem to be right. If the men had been stationed at a base, it would have been no issue at all. But because they were deployed, we couldn't join? That made no sense. Well, they did not know what they had on their hands. We were a group of upset, angry, and indignant wives of deployed officers. How dare they act as if our husbands didn't count? We made a fuss, and we threatened to make an even bigger deal out of it.

The next time we met, we were allowed to join the Picatinny Arsenal Officers' Club.

Just as I was able to find a group of women to relax with, so had the kids found friends and activities that they enjoyed. Fortunately, young Bill found his love for assembling miniature helicopters and airplanes. The kids got out of school for the summer. We would make trips to Millburn and stay a few days. Being with family was fun. These visits were relaxing, and they made the summer go faster.

When we had hot weather, we enjoyed the small Lake Picatinny in the Picatinny Arsenal. Debbie, young Bill, and Linda learned to swim while Patrick played with his toys in the sand. The arsenal also had an extraordinarily beautiful lake, Denmark, located in the mountainous region of north-central New Jersey. It had a huge fishing area where we fished and wonderful woods surrounding it.

I could also meet other women to talk with here. One day, a young officer's wife sat next to me. She was very friendly, and we got to chatting. She had just graduated from college and was telling me how car seats and belts would be mandatory someday. I thought that would never happen because our clothes would be wrinkled! Most skirts in those years were made of cotton and were starched and ironed. I have to laugh at myself now, forty-eight years later; little did I know! I was impressed with how bright and well educated this young woman was.

A few days later, one of the most wonderful things happened. Bill called from Cambodia! A terrific feeling went through my body—I was thrilled. He sounded so happy that he was hearing my voice too. As always, we said how we loved each other and couldn't wait for him to get home. He asked so many questions about the kids, making sure they were fine. What I remember the most though was hearing him say, "Doll, I love you."

He was only allowed so many minutes, and time went too fast, but it was better than no call at all. He gave me the number he was calling from so I could call back, but that didn't work.

A few weeks later, we received a box from Cambodia. The kids were so excited, and I was too. Bill sent the girls colorful dolls dressed in their customary Thailand apparel while the boys received crossbows handmade by the Viet Cong. In Vietnam, the arrow tips would have had poison on them in order to kill their enemies. They were made very skillfully out of wood and twine. While these items might have appeared to be toys, they were the real thing. All of the children were delighted with their presents from their father. These were things they would always treasure and were careful with them.

Then there were my gifts. Bill sent two exquisite rings, one black-star sapphire stone set high in gold leaves with matching earrings. The second ring was a large, higher gold setting reminiscent of a pagoda. There were three tiers of garnets starting with one at the top, seven in the middle, and twelve at the bottom. This was an almost unbelievably gorgeous piece of jewelry! I was overwhelmed with his selections. What a smart, thoughtful man I married. I call it my princess ring. In his eyes, I was his princess, and he was my prince!

The rest of the summer, we went down to Millburn a few times, plus my parents came up most weekends. The summer went by with all the activity, and I was grateful for that. It helped to occupy my time, even though nothing could keep me from constantly thinking and worrying about Bill. Time for school came again for Debbie, Bill, and Linda, but Pat had another year before he could join them.

What I had been waiting for finally occurred: Bill returned home. What a relief! I just cannot relay what an unbelievably heartwarming feeling came over me when seeing him alive and well after a long, worrisome year.

Christmas was the next month, and Bill was determined to make it the best time he could. He bought the kids a small color television and everything else that caught his eye. It was a wonderful celebration.

Fort Campbell was our next station for a year, with Bill returning to Vietnam for his second tour!

CHAPTER 27

———— ❧ ————

Fort Campbell, Kentucky (1966)

FORT CAMPBELL IS in southern Kentucky, just near the border of Tennessee. This is pretty country with plenty of hills and trees. The mountains of Tennessee are to the south of this border area with Kentucky, so instead of large vistas, there are many gently rolling hills filled with beautiful horse farms, brooks, and an abundance of trees. After the extreme mountains of Alaska and the deserts and the large trees covered with Spanish moss in the South, it was comforting to be surrounded by the lush, green tones of this temperate countryside. I thought we were very lucky to have moved into this lovely area.

Our address was 106 Robin Hood Drive, Clarksville, Tennessee, the first house in the newly built development. Street names were Maiden Marian, Little John, and more, all taken from the legend of Robin Hood and the men of Sherwood Forest. Our home was a new but modest structure. It gave us the room we needed, and it felt very comfortable. We were happy here, and Bill was commander of the airfield temporarily until a senior officer arrived.

Of course, as with any of our moves, there were always new circumstances to deal with. Debbie, young Bill, and Linda started school at the Ringgold School, traveling there by a school bus on narrow, dusty roads. It seemed like a quaint country situation. That almost idyllic feeling was shattered, however, when I was informed that the principal would paddle a student if needed! Well, that did not fly with me for one second! There was *no* way

I was going to have my children paddled in school. I marched myself into his office and made it very clear to him that neither he nor anyone else in that school system would paddle any of my children. I told him that my husband and I were perfectly capable of dealing with the disciplining of our children at home. I further insisted that he should call me if there was an issue deemed serious enough for a child to deserve corporal punishment, and I would handle that problem at home. He just sat there behind his desk and stared at me as if to say, "Where did this wild woman come from?"

After a few seconds of looking at me with a blank stare, he seemed to throw an internal switch. He was so sweet and assured me that would never happen. I suppose he was thinking in strictly legal terms that there would be no paddling or other forms of physical punishment.

Soon after that instance, young Bill came home and took off his shirt, and there were black marks on his arm where his teacher had pinched him. I could not believe what had just happened. I was outraged—I would not allow other people to harm my children. I may not be a large person, but if my children are threatened, the warrior in me emerges. Well, there we go again—this time I ignored the principal and confronted the teacher directly! She was a tiny, feisty woman, and I believe that she thought she could intimidate me. That was a serious mistake. I told her what my comments were to the principal, and I made it clear that I did not want her pinching my children nor harming them in any other way. She did not say much, but there was no more pinching after that.

We enjoyed the holidays that year immensely. We had a wonderful visit later that fall. Felice, Vince, and Suzie flew to Nashville, and we picked them up there. Nashville was not far from our home, but they enjoyed the ride through the city, which was much smaller than they expected. Then we took them north to our home through the green hills and leas of Tennessee.

They spent Thanksgiving with us, and of course, we celebrated with a traditional Thanksgiving dinner, complete with turkey, stuffing, and all the fixings. I couldn't forget pumpkin pie. But that was an added benefit to their visit. Debbie was so happy for Suzie to visit since they were the same age. Seeing the two girls being able to talk to each other and have fun with another kid their own age was very nice. For us, having family to share the holiday with was pleasant. Being with family on holidays is something that I have always enjoyed and cherished. I think it is one of the most important parts of life.

Bill drove all of us out to the mess hall on post to hear him address the troops on this holiday. He gave a nice, relaxing, short talk and got the troops laughing. Bill could do that easily. One of Bill's talents came from being a calm, laidback man; he could use his manner to get other people to relax and enjoy themselves. The soldiers probably expected a stern and formal address and were prepared for such an address. Instead, Bill spoke warmly, with humor, and with authority nevertheless. The soldiers all responded well to him. Vince, having been in the service himself years ago, really enjoyed being there with the soldiers.

We also had a bachelor officer, a friend of Bill's, over for dinner. We had single men join us often, mainly at Christmas but also for other holidays. Because they were single and usually very far from home, they enjoyed being with a family. I know Bill did before we were married. This kind of inclusion made these men feel part of a family at a time of year that could be very difficult for them otherwise.

After that visit, Christmas was near. I was so happy that this year Bill would be home for the holiday and that our family would be together. As always, there were plenty of parties to attend, plus we had the added pleasure of my parents coming down for Christmas. It was a joyous celebration—with the attending of church, the kids opening their presents, and the gathering of the family for our dinner. I loved the entire time.

Before we realized it, 1967 arrived! Knowing Bill had to return to Vietnam in the fall, time was ticking away. And I wanted to be sure to enjoy every moment with him that I could. I was dreading the time that would come when he would be deployed again to the war.

Many times Bill had to fly the generals to various places, such as Washington, DC, or many military bases for meetings. He left the house at three or four in the morning, and he could be gone for the entire day—or days at a time. I felt uneasy, and we decided it was time to buy a dog. We bought a three-month-old German shepherd from a kennel in Chicago. He came by jet airplane and arrived in Nashville. He was jet black, so naturally we named him "Jet." We all loved him.

We had a maid, Mary, who came in once a week to clean and look after Pat so I could go to the PX and commissary. She was a good maid, but she liked our gin! So we hid the good gin in the dishwasher, which was not plugged in, with a lot of stuff on top. Bill watered down another cheap gin and put it in the liquor cabinet! It seemed like a silly situation, but we did not want to have any problems because of drinking.

Pat was no problem because he could entertain himself and often spent most of the day sitting between two big limbs on the apple tree pretending he was a helicopter pilot like his dad. He idolized Bill, and he wanted to be just like his father.

Bill's replacement arrived, Lt. Col. Brooker, who outranked Bill. He introduced himself as "Lucky." He was a good man and comfortable to be around, so we were all friends almost immediately. Since he was single at the time, we had him over for dinner often and always had a good laugh. Because I was the wife of Lucky's second in command, I had some responsibilities.

I had had to fill in for a company commander's wife before, so that was fine. The women had to get their legal affairs in order. I spoke at a coffee in the Officers' Club about wills, power of attorney, insurance policies, funeral ceremonies, and other important matters. Most of these ladies did not experience their husbands going off to war with the thought that they would not return. These were all pilots' wives, and the men would be flying over enemy territory. There were many tears in the room. Thinking about these important matters isn't easy. It is, however, essential that we do; this was another uncomfortable part of being a military wife.

That was not the only talk that I gave. The next coffee topic was called "Send Your Husband to War with a Shopping List." I showed the ladies the jewelry and silk that Bill had sent plus other items. Then Lucky added to the collection. The ladies really enjoyed this meeting. After the initial talk that was so serious, it was good to relax them with something more frivolous and fun.

Bill took a week's vacation, and we drove down to Fort Benning mainly to visit Jean, Toady's wife, and some of Bill's Vietnam friends.

It was so sad to see Toady's room where he had built model ships. Most of them were the old style: tall, wooden sailboats with many sails. Yards of thin string represented ropes, with extremely intricate work. They were all masterpieces. Jean asked Bill if he would like one. Bill quickly said, "No," as I said, "Yes." Bill looked at me, slowly moving his head from side to side and softly said, "No, Doll." Later I concluded that Bill would have a difficult time having a daily remembrance of Toady in our home. I did understand then.

We had a swimming party at the Officers' Club. This would be the last time we were together in such a gathering. We gave out silly toys to the men, such as jacks, jump ropes, harmonicas, and more. It was an enjoyable evening, but it was also tinged with sadness and a bittersweet tone—the men were going to Vietnam, and most of the wives returned to their hometowns.

Meanwhile, Lucky got married to Fredia, a pretty, friendly young lady. We liked and enjoyed her. Bill and I were their witnesses. After the ceremony, we had a small group of friends over to our quarters to celebrate.

It was very important to everyone that we try to keep our lives as normal as possible, even in the face of war.

CHAPTER 28

New Jersey and Vietnam

UNFORTUNATELY, THE TIME that I had been dreading arrived. Bill would very shortly be going back for another tour of duty in Vietnam. Again, it was time to pack. Only this time, nothing went to storage. We shipped everything right to Blackwell Street, Dover. Bill would only have three weeks in Jersey before he left for Vietnam. There would be enough time to unpack everything. This was the easiest move, knowing where everything belonged.

Having Bill leave for the Vietnam tour was just as frightening as the first time. It never became any easier; I just learned to live with it.

As we saw Bill off, my knees were shaking, and I never wanted to let go of him. I wanted to kiss him one more time. Eventually though, it was time to say good-bye.

"It'll be OK, Doll," he said. "I love you."

I watched him get on the train, all the time letting my tears flow. Even though I tried to be strong, it was impossible. Again, I would be worried about Bill's safety the entire time he was gone.

It was so disturbing for children when their fathers left them to go to war in a faraway place. They try not to show their emotions on a regular day-to-day basis, but they would cry over nothing. To comfort them, I'd encourage them to cry. I did it to help them relieve the pressure and their sadness. Of course, even when we were happy on the outside, all of us were worried on the inside.

This too is part of being a military family.

Bill was stationed in ChuLai, Vietnam, with the 14th Combat Aviation Battalion XO (executive officer), south of DaNang. At this time, the Vietnam War was fully engaged with a great deal of terrible fighting occurring.

I know things were horrendous with helicopters being shot down, but Bill never wrote about what was going on except to say, "Do not watch the news." I tried very hard to listen to what he said, but it was almost impossible not to see or hear what was going on. I knew that the fighting had intensified and that the country was starting to be ripped apart by the effects of the war. It was not a good time.

At home, things were going fine. We got through another Christmas, but unlike the previous year, it was not as happy for me. I had to be the one who was completely in charge, and I felt as if I had a massive hole in my heart because I missed Bill so much. We had a hard, snowy, cold winter, complete with many days off from school for the kids, which they enjoyed.

I did have an issue to deal with now. Jet was big and had become very difficult for me to handle. I would have the leash on the dog, and when I opened the door, he pulled me down the back steps to the sidewalk. My clothes would tear, and my hands and knees would bleed. Also, Jet disliked any man in the house to the extent that I could not allow Irving, the landlord, to enter the house. One time, Jet jumped on him and went for his throat. Luckily, he did not harm him.

I took Jet to obedience classes, and he seemed to do well until he got back in our station wagon. Then he would go wild, barking and growling while jumping uncontrollably. That night, I called a kennel that bred German shepherds. When the owner came to see Jet, the dog went under the sink like a coward. I didn't know what to do. I couldn't afford to send him to obedience school for two months or more.

Several weeks later, I received a surprise phone call from Bill, calling over a hand-radio set. After every sentence, we would have to say, "Over." Bill's commented, "Doll, give Jet away and don't worry about it." I had been so emotional, and he calmed me down. Then he told me that every word I said could be heard over a loudspeaker by other soldiers waiting their turns to call home! I felt so embarrassed.

I gave Jet away to friends, one of whom was a state trooper, and he found a good home for the dog.

Bill and I hoped to meet in Hawaii when he completed the first nine months in Vietnam. Mom and Dad would stay at my house to take care of our four kids, except for young Bill. My sister, Marie, was kind enough to keep Bill with them in Millburn. That way he could fish with Uncle Billy. Young Bill didn't misbehave, but he was a torment to his siblings. The other kids were quiet and laidback. Bill was a talker and always on the move.

A few days before I was to leave, Debbie came down with an ear infection. We had been swimming a lot up at the lake.

The day came for me to leave, and it was difficult leaving the kids, most of all Debbie. She was medicated for swimmer's ear, and I was going halfway around the world.

Thank God for my good friend and neighbor, Barbara Bettons. She also was an RN and assured me she would keep checking on Debbie.

I finally left, trying not to cry, waving as Barbara's husband, Ronney, drove to the Newark airport. Well, flying out of Newark in those days was a nightmare. Ronney walked to the gate with me. From there the passengers were shunted along, like a huge herd of cattle, and squeezed into a very small area encased in six-foot or higher barbed wire. Being short, I could not see Ronney or even get my arm up to wave. What an unpleasant way to start a long trip.

The flight from Newark, New Jersey, to Los Angeles, California, was fine. Boarding for Hawaii, I met many service wives who were meeting their husbands. We all had so much to talk about, and we connected so well. Being able to have long conversations with women who were in the same situation was comforting. We were all in the same difficult boat in very choppy waters and worried about our husbands together.

The flight was smooth and without any problems. When we were over Hawaii, the view was spectacular as we looked down at the islands. The radiant sunshine seemed to be brighter than any I had seen anywhere else. It flooded the plane and cast a golden glow on the islands below. With the crystal-clear blue ocean surrounding the bits of green that made up the islands, the whole view was breathtaking! In fact, it was sublime.

The landing was perfect.

After a taxi ride to the Ilaki Hotel, I began to relax. I was excited and nervous, and I was so anxious to see my husband. I couldn't wait to finally be with Bill again. But I had to. If I could only sleep, it would have helped, but that never happened.

Our large room was on the highest floor except for the famous restaurant on the top floor, featuring the magnificent view of the boats and ocean waves. We had the same view from our balcony, plus a sitting area, kitchenette, and bedroom, including a pretty Hawaiian lei made of flowers arranged for us on the bed pillows. When I looked out, I could see the marina with what looked like hundreds of beautiful yachts and boats secured and waiting to be used at sea. The ocean was calm and a deep blue that seemed to have come from the palette of a celestial painter. It was almost too beautiful to be believed.

Now for the long wait! I had no idea when Bill would appear. It was late afternoon when I arrived, so I unpacked, showered, put on something more comfortable, and started to wait and wait and wait some more. It seemed as if I would have to wait forever.

At 2 a.m., I heard the key turn in the lock, and my tall, handsome husband in his uniform stood there. I ran to him as he did the same. As he wrapped his strong arms around me, tears ran down my face as he kept kissing me. I felt as if I was melting, as if this were the first time we kissed, the last time we kissed, and each time we kissed. We stood there, hanging on to each other for the longest time, trying to believe we were together. We had been away from each other for so long but only in physical terms. In reality, we were never truly separated from each other.

As soon as we could figure out the time difference, Bill called home to talk with the kids, mainly Debbie, to hear how she was feeling. She told him she was better while she crying with happiness that she could talk to her dad. He talked to Linda and Patrick also, and Mom and Dad. It was heartwarming and satisfying.

Every day we would meet many old friends from flight school and other army posts. It was like old-home week. We had so much to talk about—their children, where they had been stationed, what they had seen, and what their lives were like. It was almost like a reunion. It was so much fun. The time went by so fast. Many of us would gather by the pool. One afternoon we sat poolside listening to a combo rehearsing "Sunrise, Sunset," our favorite song. It was very romantic. We even got up and slow danced. I was so happy that day.

One evening a group of us enjoyed Don Ho, the famous Hawaiian singer. He had a low, soft, soothing voice. He slowly walked between the tables, singing and shaking hands with the servicemen and thanking them for their services. It was a nice, relaxing show.

We also spent an afternoon with Wally Blasdell, but we didn't get to see Aloma or Karlin. Wally, a native Hawaiian, gave us a marvelous tour of the island. We saw the sugar-cane fields and then drove through the mountains' bright-green foliage. These were immense spans of green stalks waving like ocean waves over the ground. And some of the fields had stalks that went over six or seven feet into the air. What a magnificent and beautiful sight those fields were!

Wally pointed out the Hawaiian anthurium plant in many colors. The Hawaiians call it the "Little Boy Flower." Its dominant color was a brilliant red, and it seemed to fill the fields with a burning brilliance.

We also were shown the mountains and volcanoes. I was delighted to see some of the most unusual, powerful, and beautiful sights I had ever had the good fortune to witness. This was nature at its grandest, and a huge palm tree seemed to tower above everything. With its enormous bright-green leaves, I felt small in its presence.

During this entire trip, Bill slept very little because he didn't want to waste the time. He wanted to experience as much as possible; even during downtime, when he watched television, which really relaxed him, he got a laugh out of the commercials. After nine months without a TV, it all looked good. Standing out on the balcony and listening to the ocean waves was so calming for him. I am sure he needed this even more than I did after being in Vietnam. And we both needed this time together.

One morning Bill woke me up, saying, "Doll, you have to see this." It was still dark, and he could not figure out why he saw the headlights from cars driving on the sand at the ocean's edge. Then the lights went off. What were they doing in the dark? As it became a little lighter, we could see the cars leaving. We finally figured it out—people were surf boarding. How about that? It was clear that we were tourists.

What a marvelous week this had been. It was like a second honeymoon, but it had to end. Bill left the following Saturday in the early evening. After this wonderful week, it was so hard to see him leave. But Bill was concerned about me flying home, and I worried about him returning to war. As always, because we were both so in love with each other, we were each more worried about the other than about ourselves, which I think is one of the definitions of true love.

As Bill stood in the elevator, he tried to hold the door from closing to kiss me one more time. Finally, though, we had the last kiss, and he had to leave.

That was a long, lonely night in that big room. The next morning, I got on the same elevator. As the door closed, there was Bill's handprint on the shiny door! My heart sank.

I was happy to get on my flight the next day to San Francisco where our Yuma Test Station friends were meeting me. As I got off the plane, Ginny and Bill Rainscuk were approaching me. Ginny was in a black, full-length winter coat because it was cold in Northern California. There I was in a light-blue linen suit and freezing. Thoughtfully, Ginny had brought a blanket, so I wrapped myself up when I got into their car. They were stationed at the Presidio army post in Monterey, California.

Visiting with their family was a treat, having a delicious dinner and talking nonstop. It was a great relief to me and diverted my attention from the reality that Bill had just left for Vietnam again. I needed to have my mind occupied.

The next morning as Ginny was driving to the airport, I saw peace signs. "Love children" were holding them. The beatniks had headbands on plus plenty of beads around their necks and wrists. They were singing softly as they strolled along. What an incredible sight and a reminder how divided the country was at that time!

At this point, I was so anxiously waiting to see the kids. I needed to be with them. We had four months, and then Bill would be home, God willing! It didn't sound like a long time, but each day of separation from Bill was a torment because I didn't know if he was safe or not, if he was hurt or worse. I didn't want to think about it, but not thinking about it was impossible.

Arriving home, I found we had more members of the family: goldfish. Barb and Ronney took Linda and Patrick to the town carnival while Debbie and Mom stayed at their home to care for baby Michael. The kids were so excited that they had won the goldfish at one of the children's game booths.

It was truly wonderful seeing the kids; it looked as if they all had grown in that short time. My mother was there, and she even had Ella and Hen over for dinner one evening. That surprised me and made me happy. It was good to see harmony in the extended family.

It was fall, and Bill's sister, Peggy, was at risk of having a miscarriage with her fourth pregnancy. She was frightened naturally, so I took care of Jeffery, her happy roly-poly baby who loved to eat and was not walking yet. He was a delightful baby and very easy to care for, and the kids loved him.

Peggy's husband delivered Jeff to me Sunday night and picked him up on Friday night. We loved having him, and he took the war off our minds.

This routine went on for several weeks until I ruptured two disks in my lower back. I could barely move. I could not sit, felt terrible lying down, and could only function a bit if I stood. The pain was intense. Ella and Hen came to watch over Jeff. I got an appointment with an orthopedic physician up the hill from me. Before I left, standing at the kitchen table, I ate a Jersey beefsteak-and-tomato sandwich. The tomatoes completely covered the bread. I was able to enjoy this sandwich even though I was in deep pain. I finally made it up to the office ever so slowly.

The doctor immediately gave me a shot to relieve the pain, but it completely paralyzed me! I couldn't even speak; I could only blink my eyes! I threw up my delicious sandwich, but I could not spit any of it out of my mouth, and there was a real danger that I could choke to death. The nurse moved into action quickly and swabbed my mouth out. This all happened while I sat in a chair. I don't know how the nurses managed to get me up on the examining table because I was dead weight.

I kept praying to God, "Please don't let me die here, with Bill in Vietnam."

I kept looking at the clock, uneasy about Pat in school in Dover, where he could be stranded. Debbie, Bill, and Linda walked home from school so that was a plus. I felt as if I was in this condition for hours, and I was scared to death. I finally started to move, and as soon as I could talk, I had the nurse call Ella so she would pick up Pat. Later Ella and then all the kids came to get me. I was so happy and relieved that I had recovered the ability to move and speak, thanking God under my breath. I spent days on the couch with my legs propped up on pillows.

Debbie took over and did an excellent job. She wanted to sleep on the floor next to me in case I needed anything. I thought she should sleep in her bed since she had to get the kids up and off to school. I kept Pat home from school since I couldn't drive. We were all sorry we could not take care of Jeff anymore.

For the longest time, I wore a brace for my back. It reminded me of years past when ladies wore corsets to hold their stomachs flat; it was laced up the front with metal stays. That's what I wore; I laced it and then pulled the strings in order to make it very tight, holding my back straight. It was such an odd feeling, but I know that it helped me to deal with this back problem. Again, I could have used Bill during this time.

Marie and Billy brought young Bill home to me. He had had a delightful time, of course. She had treated him like a king, fixing his favorite food and sending him fishing with Uncle Billy. I am sure this became a lifelong cherished memory for young Bill. Debbie, Bill, and Linda continued school at St. Mary's along with Patrick, who was in his first year of school.

By mid-October, Bill was promoted to lieutenant colonel, with a silver leaf. We were happy that was approved. It was a wonderful achievement and promotion for him. He also received orders for a six-month tour at Army Staff College in Norfolk, Virginia. We were extremely happy with those orders. Now all we had to do was to get him home safely.

We would have to put our furniture back in storage because the quarters in Norfolk were furnished.

The rest of the time was like a slow-motion blur, with the kids occupied with homework and play and me thinking about the next move and Christmas and counting the days until Bill's return.

Finally, Bill was home! My beloved husband was back safe, and our children's father was home, halleluiah! There would be no more going off to war! Bill had done his duty to his country, had served in Vietnam honorably and bravely, and could finally continue his military career back in the United States of America.

Understandably, after the kind of stress he had been through in war, Bill just wanted to spend some time relaxing and goofing off. Plus, he was happy to see relatives and friends. We were only home for about two weeks. Our Christmas was perfect, and by the first week in January, we were packed again and on the road south.

Dover, New Jersey

Bill- Chu La, Vietman - 1968

Hawaii - 1968

CHAPTER 29

———— ✧ ————

Armed Forces Staff College, Norfolk, Virginia

WHEN WE FIRST learned of this move, Bill and I had pictured a campus setting, with old ivy-covered buildings, bucolic passageways, and a well-manicured quad. Much to our surprise, the college was surrounded by high barbed wire with armed soldiers walking the perimeter of the college twenty-four hours. The mission of the Joint Armed Forces Staff College is to educate national security professionals in planning and executing joint, multination, and interagency operations in order to install a primary commitment to joint, multinational, and interagency teamwork, attitudes, and perspectives. So this was not a place to find undergraduates throwing Frisbees outside, carrying paperbacks in their jeans pockets, or several youngsters sitting around discussing philosophy.

We arrived in Norfolk two weeks early in order for Bill to get some flying time. Pilots had a required flight time to fill. Bill reported to the flight surgeon to have a flight examination. He found out he had an ear infection, which made flying impossible for him. Instead, we would check out the area and maybe do a little unwinding.

Unfortunately, the weather did not cooperate with our plans. We had a two-bedroom hotel looking over the ocean, which did not give much room for children's activities, and it rained every day. Thank goodness, the kids had their own TV. This at least gave them the chance to watch children's shows, and that occupied some of their time. Because of the kids' boredom, we took them out in the rain so they could run in the wet sand. They were surprised that we allowed it, but they had a good time running around and burning off some of their energy. They ran, jumped, and even ran a bit into the edge of the cold ocean, and they squealed and laughed in delight. We all came in cold and wet, but it was well worth it just to exercise a little.

We finally moved into our well-furnished apartment. I was surprised at how nice it was. It was reasonably large and had essentially everything we needed. This was a major but very pleasant change from the hotel we had been staying in. Also, there was a nice mixture of people because every branch of service was represented there.

It took a little while for Bill to get accustomed to schoolwork, but it was a good change that he needed. He had been very used to being a man of action on the field and in a helicopter; now, he had to be a man of the mind and one who would be taking lessons and instructing others.

The kids attended Granby Elementary School, except Debbie, who went to the middle school. For the kids, who had become used to sudden changes, this was not a big deal at all. They dealt with it with humor and good attitudes.

On weekends, we had plenty to do and see in this historic area. Most of the time, we could tour the large ships and submarines that were anchored in Norfolk. The sailors loved having visitors, especially the children. They were gracious and welcoming, and they would engage the kids in conversation about the beautiful ships. I guess we reminded them of home.

A wonderful event that occurred was connected with our extended family.

On a sunny day, January 23, 1969, Tami Gelpke was baptized in a tiny chapel on the *John F. Kennedy* aircraft carrier docked in Norfolk, Virginia. Eddy Gelpke, E-5, weatherman, stationed on the *JFK*, is my first cousin, married to Vira, and Tami was their third girl.

The families came down from New Jersey for Tami's christening. It so happened to be Aunt Florence's (Freddy's mother) birthday, our fifteenth wedding anniversary, and my mother's birthday on the twenty-fifth; so the very pleasant synchronicity magnified the family gathering.

At the baptism, the minister passed this tiny one-week-old baby to a sailor to hold and then on to the next sailor until they all had held Tami. It was a beautiful sight and a very memorable experience!

The *John F. Kennedy* was a massive ship. Walking through that handsome vessel was a big thrill. While I walked on this huge ship, it was easy for me to imagine what it would be like at sea. We had a grand family reunion later. Tami's name is now in the National Archives because she was the first baby to be baptized aboard the *JFK*. How terrific is that!

This tour was a vacation for me. There were so many historical homes around and of course, in Williamsburg, Virginia. Once warm weather hit, we would head for Dam Neck, a large beach area on the Atlantic Ocean just for military families. We bought the kids rubber rafts to ride the waves. They were not too large and perfect for them. Most of our new friends went there with their kids too, and this gave us the opportunity to get to know one another. After Patrick had a full day in the ocean and playing in the sand, he was a little reluctant to join his father in the bathhouse for a shower. He said that he did not want those men looking at his bare butt! The day was fun, most of all for Bill, having just returned from Vietnam and needing this kind of family getaway. Bill also had a pleasant surprise when he met a man he served with in Vietnam.

Felice, Vince, and their son, Bruce, stopped to see us on their way home to New Jersey from Bruce's graduation from St. Andrews College in Lauringburg, North Carolina. Naturally, we took them to visit the Norfolk Ship Yard. Bruce noticed an interesting sight. There was a new nuclear submarine tied next to an old conventional sub. The newer sub was much bigger and ran on diesel. They enjoyed the afternoon.

The six months went so swiftly. Given that we all loved the beach, it made the time pass quickly and easily, but it seemed that change was the one constant that we always lived with. Bill received orders for Fort Belvoir, Virginia, not far from Washington, DC.

Just like before, we called our army friends, Jan and Dave Dukes from Ft. Richardson, Alaska. They knew a family who wanted to rent their house for one year, and Jan assured us the house was perfect. The elementary school was just down the street, and they were close by. Having been reassured, I felt very comfortable with making our plans for this move.

Army friends are the best people anyone could ever find.

So we were off again. This was an easy move.

CHAPTER 30

Fort Belvoir, Virginia

WE MOVED TO Springfield, Virginia, an active, small town in 1969 outside of Fort Belvoir. This particular relocation was one of the easiest we had ever experienced, which was a relief. The house was everything Jan said it would be. It was a pretty home, in excellent shape, and the owner kept lovely flowerbeds, which thrilled me. The house itself suited us, and I was thrilled with the ease of this move. We moved in, but our household goods did not arrive for a couple of days.

We didn't have any furniture except the rubber rafts, which the children slept on. We also had beach chairs the Dukes gave us, as well as two army cots and blankets. The kids all settled in for the night. The next morning, I looked in at the girls. They were nowhere to be seen. I yelled to Bill, "The girls are gone!" As he appeared, I opened the closet door, and there they were, all squeezed up together. The mats kept sliding on the waxed hard floor, so this was their solution.

On July 20, 1969, we all sat in front of a little TV on the beach chairs or the floor watching Neil Armstrong stand on the moon. Here was an event of the greatest significance to the human race. We had finally been able to make the ultimate exploration to a place away from our native Earth, and we were all watching as if we were on the beach on vacation. This was a magnificent moment for all of humanity.

In many ways, this move was very good for us. Not only did it signal that Bill was definitely not going back to war, but it brought us closer physically to our families and to several old friends.

Bill's best man, Bert, had married my bridesmaid, Jean, and they lived in Leonard Town, Maryland, high on the Potomac River banks. Being so close to them was wonderful. We had lunch sitting in their kitchen and looking down on that massive river. We had a postcard picture with a spectacular view of tobacco fields and the many ships of all types traveling the river. Jean remarked that she ruined many meals looking out the window. We would visit back and forth for the rest of the year. The kids had a wild time being driven in and out of the tobacco fields. Huge pastures of the green plants went for miles.

Bill attended US Army Management School, which took up much of his time. Afterward, he was involved in the project designing the airplane/helicopter named the Cheyenne. He was very excited about the prospect, since he could fly both kinds of aircraft.

It was hard to believe how quickly the time had passed. Our children were no longer little ones toddling around; instead, they were growing up rapidly. Debbie went to Springfield High School, while young Bill attended Washington Irving Middle School. Linda and Patrick walked two blocks to Lynbrook Elementary School. But not everything was cheerful.

We had a huge shock when Bill's dad died suddenly in January. We drove up to New Jersey immediately, and it was a very sad time for all of us. Of course, all of the family and numerous friends were there. Bill took it hard, but as always, he was strong for those around him who needed it.

However, Bill soon after requested that his next assignment would be Picatinny Arsenal, Dover, New Jersey.

While Bill served at Fort Belvoir, we attended some parties, but they were nothing like Fort Hood. I was active with the Officers' Club Wives' Club coffees and luncheons. I always enjoyed the ladies and the locations of these events.

This sounds genteel and sophisticated, but life was a bit more adventurous than that.

We had a snowstorm with a hard crust of ice on top, but the children's schools were still in session. Linda and Pat had already left for school, but then I remembered something. I was about to step into the shower when all of a sudden, I thought, "Did they remember their lunch money on the dining-room table?" No, the money was still there. I slipped into snow boots that should have shoes in them first! I only had on a short shower robe and a knee-length winter coat. And off I went, walking, half running down the street to school, slipping, sliding, and slopping as I hurried along. I was standing on the sidewalk until I could cross over to the school. I went to jump over the icy snow bank. As I jumped, the boots stayed in the snow, my feet flew out of them, and I went flying down! I went face down, arms spread out! My coat flew up, and I knew my derriere had to be showing because an eighteen-wheeler sounded out a few honks from the truck's horn. I was able to stand up to go to retrieve my boots. I tried to be nonchalant, as if I had planned that! Every step I took, I'd go deeper into the icy snow before I could reach my ice-filled boots. I did reach them, and with as much finesse as I could muster, I put them on. Finally, I pulled myself together, hopeful that none of the neighbors saw me dragging myself home. That little tale, of course, was not army related, but anytime Springfield, Virginia, comes to mind, I think of that crazy day, and I have to laugh too! Does *I Love Lucy* come to mind?

Once in the house, I headed for the shower. My feet were like two bricks of ice, and my kneecaps were bleeding as were the palms of my hands. After school, each one of the kids asked me how I scratched my face. I just said very calmly, "Oh, I just fell in the snow." None of them said anymore. I guess since I was up walking and talking things were normal. Also, when I mentioned they forgot their money, one of them said something like the teacher gave us the money and we can pay her tomorrow. "Don't worry, Mom." That was nice of her. Amen.

When I told Bill the story, he first wanted to know if I was OK. Then he couldn't help laughing, and I did too.

Finally, the winter broke; although, I have to say that it was mild in comparison to what we had experienced in Alaska. Nevertheless, I was still happy to see the oncoming blooming of flowers and the emerging green on the trees. This area was so beautiful in the springtime, and with the coming of that season of rebirth, we had many visitors. Even Marie's daughter, Kathleen, came down with her girlfriend, Linda. We also spent many weekends up in Wharton to check on Ella.

Bill had six weeks left of this tour, and our lease was expiring. We were blessed again; our friends across the street were planning on vacationing in England for a month. Yet again, we put all our household furniture and belongings into storage and rented their house. In addition to renting from them, we also took care of their big, orange tabby cat named Maraduke and two gerbils. That silly cat would bite my ankles every morning when I would open the door, so I quickly jumped on a dining room chair. I passed that job on to Bill.

When we left there, we went to a hotel with a large swimming pool for two weeks. This felt as if we were staying in real luxury, so we enjoyed every moment of it. By the time we left Virginia, we all had dark tans.

Then it was time for us to move on to Picatinny Arsenal and Wharton, New Jersey. We had made a full circle!

CHAPTER 31

Picatinny Arsenal, Dover, New Jersey

WHEN I SAW our new quarters, number 1127, I thought, "Just let me live in this house forever." It was one of the older homes, probably built before the arsenal's existence. It was set back from the main road. It had a large, screened-in porch, an extra-large living room with a fireplace, a spacious dining room, a kitchen, a powder room, and a small den. Upstairs, there were three big bedrooms and a bathroom. I was so happy with this new home.

Bill drove about a half mile to his office in the headquarters building. He was the United States Combat Developments Command liaison officer to headquarter US Army Munitions Command, Dover, New Jersey. That sure is a mouthful. He would travel to Washington, DC, every so often. It was an impressive title and a very important position. I was very proud of Bill, not simply because he was my husband but because he was such a good soldier and officer, and he had earned this position.

Debbie attended Morris Knolls High School in Denville, New Jersey. She went on a school bus. I always thought this sight was funny. Every school day a large army staff car would drive down our lane to pick up young Bill, Linda, and Patrick (all I could see were the three little heads) and drive them to St. Mary's School. Later in the afternoon that would be done in reverse.

Summer was a fun time at the pool or going to the Jersey shore. Bill and Debbie went deep-sea fishing and loved it. There was always a picnic going on in Millburn. Bill started to play golf;

the arsenal had a grand golf course. Young Bill soon joined his dad.

When the kids realized Bill actually was going to retire, Debbie said to Patrick, "You poor guy; you'll spend the rest of your life going to the same school."

In the fall, we were invited by our West Point friend to enjoy watching a football game at the Point. Watching the cadets in full dress uniforms as they marched out of the tunnels with the enormous old, stone buildings beyond them was such a pleasant experience. It was a grand sight and a very good day!

Our social life was full. We were invited to many Christmas parties given by friends. These events kept us very busy and happy over the holidays.

In return for all of this wonderful hospitality, we decided to return the favor. Bill and I, as well as Mae and Frank Healy, gave a St. Patrick's Day party at the Officers' Club with a full buffet, open bar, green beer, and Irish music. Many people attended, and all had a great time.

Joining the various organizations had many benefits. We even joined the Garden Club, so we had our own flowerbed in the Officers' Greenhouse. This was a fun group of people.

The Women's Club acquired a bus in order to drive the ladies to New York City to see a live show of Regis Philbin and Kathy Lee. We were late, so we had to enter the show during the commercial time. When we all walked in, Regis came running to us and said, "Where have you been?" as if we were family! He kissed a few of us on the cheek. How about that? It was a thrill for the day!

But other events balanced the fun we were having. Life is also filled with responsibilities.

Ella had a few mini strokes and was in and out of the hospital. We finally persuaded her to move in with us at the arsenal. She was contented and happy to be with the kids. We were able to care for her and give her as much comfort as we could. Ella died in February 1972, but she died in the embrace of her family.

She was a huge loss for Bill, naturally. Now Bill and I had the job of cleaning out her home of some fifty-plus years. It took us months since it was winter. We finally accomplished that deed so that it could be rented. I am sure it was often difficult and sad for Bill to go through Ella's accumulated belongings, but as always, he was a strong man.

On the Saturday afternoon before Easter, Gen. Graham, commander of Picatinny Arsenal, knocked on our front door. He was holding two beautiful orchids for my mother and me to wear to church. The general had a hothouse connected to his quarters and raised orchids. He was so pleasant. We all admired him and Mrs. Graham. They were casual people; therefore, we could be relaxed with them. He sat and talked to Mom and Dad for a while, and then he left. The general was definitely one of a kind. I never heard of a two-star general just stopping by. It was "outstanding" (Bill's favorite word)!

Then I started to house hunt since Bill would retire that summer. Bill always admired a house on Dewey Avenue while he traveled that road to bowl. One night after bowling, he came home excited, saying, "Doll, my house is for sale. Tomorrow, go buy it!"

Laughing, I said, "What if we don't like it?"

His reply was "We will change it."

So we bought 358 Dewey Avenue the next night! How is that for good fortune?

CHAPTER 32

Retirement, New Jersey

WE HAD A grand farewell with parties and Bill's retirement ceremony, which was very touching but sad also. Bill's work for his adult life had been serving the country in the military, and now he was moving on from that career. He was presented with a framed, wooden, senior aviator's wings representing the silver senior wings with a star, which was worn on his uniform as Lt. Col. William J. Gorman, infantry.

Upon his retirement after twenty years of service, Bill was awarded The Legion of Merit for exceptionally meritorious conduct in the performance of outstanding service. He achieved the rank of lieutenant colonel. He completed a tour of duty in Korea from August 1955 through December 1956 and two tours in Vietnam from August 1965 through August 1966 and November 1967 through October 1968. He was awarded three Bronze Stars for meritorious achievement in ground operations against hostile forces and four Air Medals for meritorious achievement while participating in aerial flight. He also received the Army Commendation Medal, two National Defense Service Medals, the Armed Forces Reserve Medal, the Vietnam Service Medal, and the Republic of Vietnam Campaign medal with "60" device.

I really liked being an army wife; no matter how many times we moved, it was always a stimulating challenge that made life interesting. And we did move twenty-seven times! I was always asking Bill where he thought we would go next time.

This time our move was to our civilian life!

Bill's Medals

Bill's Master pilot wings

Bill's Retirement

Heliport dedicated

Photo by Robert Eberle

A State Police medical helicopter lands at Morristown Memorial Hospital's new heliport atop the Jefferson Building. The landing pad was dedicated yesterday to the memory of the late William Gorman, hospital director of security from 1971 to 1986 and an Army officer who flew a helicopter during the Vietnam War. The hospital's original heliport was closed in 1989 due to construction.

THE STAR LEDGER   JUNE 15, 1991

Dedication – June 15, 1991

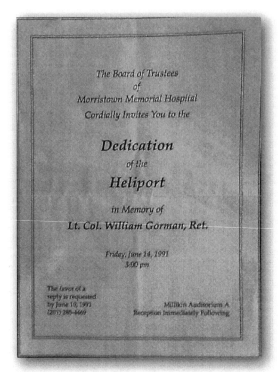

Invitation to Dedication

Marie, me and Felice

Claire and Aunt Mae

CHAPTER 33

———— ❧ ————

After Retirement

BILL TOOK A few months off before trying to find a job; we still had college costs looking at us. Later, Bill was employed by Morristown Memorial Hospital as assistant director of security in Morristown, New Jersey. I also found a perfect office job working in town for North Jersey Acoustics, a ceiling installer, and two grand and thoughtful gentlemen, David Whitmore and Frank Sullivan. Both of our boys worked for them during school breaks.

The years passed; college was paid, and we both retired. Bill officially retired from the hospital on January 1, 1987. The hospital held a farewell dinner party for him.

It was Bill's fifty-seventh birthday when he came down with flu-type symptoms. He had a high temperature and perspired profusely. Later in the evening, he began to hallucinate that he was back in the war, telling me to look out for the bombs. He was admitted to Dover General Hospital that night. The following day, the ambulance from Morristown General Hospital arrived to transport him there, where he had worked. Many people from the hospital had sought Bill's advice on both work and personal matters. They kidded him about being "Mr. Anthony" from an old radio program, in which Mr. Anthony solved questions of almost any kind.

Unknown infections ran rampant throughout his body and affected his ability to communicate. Our only communication was when I would take his hand and say, "Hi, honey."

He would reply, "Hi, love," nearly opening his eyes. Bill had the very best specialist, every test known to medical science was taken, and the best medications were given, but to no avail. The love of my life died two months later on March 26, 1987.

Linda was with me most of the time. My sister, Felice, flew in from California and stayed with me for five weeks while Bill was in the hospital. I will always show my appreciation to her for her thoughtfulness. My sincere thanks, also, to the Morristown Memorial Hospital staff for their teamwork and compassion.

After the funeral, with four priests on the altar celebrating Mass at St. Mary's Church, Bill was laid to rest with the traditional army protocol with a twenty-one-gun salute and "Taps." When that was played, the sound and emotion went right through me. Then I was presented with an American flag. It was both touching and heart rending.

Everyone was then invited to the Picatinny Arsenal Officers' Club for lunch. It was a very sad day.

June 15, 1991

On this day, a heliport on the top of the Jefferson Building at Morristown Memorial was dedicated "in the memory of Bill." Only emergency medical helicopters would land here. The dedication was held in the hospital auditorium. My family and friends and the hospital employees were there. The room was packed to standing room only.

Many of us went up to the heliport. The state police were kind enough to have a medevac helicopter fly and land right in front of us. That was a thrill.

Everyone was invited to our home for refreshments.

Bill would have been proud!

Epilogue

THE ARMY BRATS turned out incredibly well. Debi resides in New Mexico with her husband, Tom. She is an RN and the quality manager at the local hospital. They have two grown children, Christopher and Corein, and my great-grandchild, Abby.

Bill resides in Maryland with his wife, Kim. He is a CPA for a national firm. They have four children: Erin, Kate, Ford, and Alex.

Linda lives in Pennsylvania with her husband, Dennis. She owns her own holistic practice. They have three grown sons: Brian, Kurt, and Clint.

Patrick resides in Connecticut. After twenty-five years of combined service as a helicopter pilot with the United States Army and United States Coast Guard, he retired as a commander in the United States Coast Guard. Currently, he is a production test pilot with Sikorsky Aircraft. He has two grown sons: Patrick and Joe.

The Gorman Family - 2014

My Heartfelt Thanks

To GOD FOR giving me life.

To the blessed mother Mary for her powerful Rosary.

To my husband Bill for his unconditional love.

To my children, Debi, Bill, Linda, and Patrick, for their love and abundance of endless joy.

To my family, friends, and old army buddies for allowing me to pick their memory banks:

Buck and LaDonna Rogers
Ben and Dianne Anderson
Bill and Ginny Rainscuk
Dora Thurman
Mary Harris
Joe Adducci, MD

To my faithful typists, proofreaders, and illustrator.

To my book club, Happy Bookies Eating Cookies, for their encouragement to write *My Life as an Army Wife.*

With much love and gratitude,
Edy

Edythe Price Gorman

I WAS BORN in 1929, during the Great Depression. The third daughter of a factory worker and a seamstress, we lived in Millburn, a small suburb, outside of Newark, New Jersey. I contracted rheumatic fever as a child and spent a year completely bedridden. Amazingly, I survived and attended Wyoming Elementary, and went on to graduate from Millburn High School class of 1948. A social, but naive young lady, I left my family and community and embarked on a journey of unknowns when I married Second Lieutenant, Bill Gorman, US Army on January 23, 1954!! That's when I became a proud army wife.

Made in the USA
Middletown, DE
16 October 2016